"me 'n Henry"

Walter Swan

"me 'n Henry"

A story about two boys growing up on the old family homestead in Cochise County when Arizona was an infant state.

BY WALTER SWAN

ISBN 0-927176-05-X

SWAN ENTERPRISES
P.O. Box 4309
Bisbee, AZ 85603

Printed by
Skyline Printing Co., Inc.
Tucson, Arizona

This book is
dedicated
to my many family
members and friends
who have given
their support and
encouragement over
the many years this
book has been in
preparation.
And, especially, to
my wife who had to
learn to use the
computer so she could
typeset and design
this book.

CONTENTS

INTRODUCTION

HOW IT ALL GOT STARTED

"Daddy, will you tell me a story about when you were a little boy about my size? A really – happen story, 'cause they're a lot better than the other kind." And this is how it all got started.

You see, I was the father of a big family. At least, it seemed so to me and my wife. There were eight kids, four boys and four girls, and among them there were two sets of twins. So this put them all real close together.

I spent most of my time a finding something for them to eat and to wear and my wife spent most of her time a washing diapers and taking care of them in general. There was not too much money or time left over after that was done, but there was a lot of love there and we were all very happy.

One of the fun times was in the evening. That was a time when we were all together. My good wife would pop a big dishpan full of popcorn and pour a lot of good homemade butter on it and the bigger boys would get some wood for the fireplace. We'd build a big fire and I would stretch out on the floor with two or three kids heads pillowed on my arms. Then I would tell them a story or

11

two before bedtime while my wife sat in the rocking chair and rocked the babies to sleep.

One evening, after supper, while all of the kids were outside a playing, my wife, Deloris, said to me, "Do you realize that you have lived in a day that is real choice, back when there were more horses on the street than there were cars, up to the time of TV and all of the modern conveniences we have today? I think you should write your experiences down so that when our kids grow up, their kids can see what it was like when you were a kid."

"But, Mama," I protested, "You know how hard it is for me to spell, much less write, and no one can read it when I write, even you, so how would that be possible?"

She answered, "I don't know, Sweetheart, but it would be nice if you could do it."

Now this was back in 1952 when all of this started. Well, I got out the portable typewriter that we had bought for the kids to do their homework on and I started in. It was a real struggle at first. It took a long time to even get one page typed, but as I went along, it got a lot easier.

We had a file cabinet and whenever I would type out a story my wife would put it in that file cabinet in a folder labeled "Daddy's Stories" and somehow that file kept a growing and a growing. It's 1988 now and that one file has grown into several files.

I am forever grateful to my wife for the many hours she has spent typing and correcting all of the misspelled words. ·And now it is my hope, that as you read this book you will feel, as I felt, what it was like back when there were not so many conveniences and modern things to make life easier for us.

CHAPTER 1

BEFORE ME 'N HENRY

Our Father

Our father, Albert Jackson Swan, arrived in Bisbee, Arizona at the turn of the century with his father, Henry Hunting Swan, his mother, Elizabeth Caroline Jackson Swan, and his brother, Clarence. Uncle Clarence had tuberculos – is. They heard that the dry Arizona climate was supposed to be good for TB people and that is why they had all moved there from east Texas. My Dad was twenty – four or five.

Most all of the government land was already home – steaded. However, there was one location that my father liked real well. On checking the county courthouse records, he found that this one hundred sixty acres was not filed on yet. So he filed on it before he left Tombstone, which was the county seat at the time. It was some twenty – five miles away, so that meant a good day's ride on horseback.

Grandpa Swan filed on the one hundred sixty acre spot right north of my dad's new homestead.

Daddy got a job at the Southern Pacific Railroad

13

"me 'n Henry"

Our father, Albert Jackson Swan

The old Osborn Depot

Daddy's shack on his old homestead.

depot some mile and a half away from his new homestead,
handling the Railway Express. In those days, this
was known as the Osborn Station, but since it has been
changed to the name of Bisbee Junction.

The first thing a person on a new homestead needs is
a place to live and water and the only way to get water
was to dig a well and that isn't so easy to do sometimes.
It was a long slow process. It takes several months when
you have to dig it yourself with a pick and shovel.
Sometimes even longer when you get down so deep that you
can't throw the dirt out with the shovel. Then you have
to put the dirt in a bucket and draw it out a bucketful at
a time.

My dad got some help from Uncle Clarence, but he was
not much help because of his TB.

Daddy worked ten hours a day, six days a week at the
railroad depot. Once in a while, when work was sort of
slow, he got off to work on his well, and he always looked
forward to this.

When he had the well some thirty feet deep he figured
that he was about to get water any day. Most of the wells
around there struck water at about that depth.

One morning he got up early to work in the well. He
walked down to the well and as he got to the edge of it,
something happened and he lost his balance and fell to the
bottom of that dark hole.

As soon as he hit the bottom, he knew that he had
landed on his right foot on top of a big boulder that had
been left there from the day before. He looked at his
foot and saw that he had a badly crushed ankle.

Just as luck would have it, there was no one close
around to give him any help, especially that time of the
morning. It was beginning to hurt him real bad. He
looked at the top of the well and it was just getting
daylight.

"How in the world will I ever get out of here?" he

said to himself.

At that moment something brushed his face. He lifted
his hand to brush it away and discovered that it was a
rope. He had knocked it in when he fell. He pulled hard
on it to see if it was fastened solid enough to hold him,
hoping the other end wouldn't go through the pulley. But
it held fast, that is, for the time being. The only hope
he had was to climb the rope hand over hand and hope that
it would hold until he got to the top. The longer he
waited, the more pain he was in.

His next big worry was, could he make it to the top
without fainting from the pain and falling back down
again? But he had to try. It was the only way.

He used the foot that was not hurt to help himself
keep away from the side of the well. There were several
times on the way up that he thought that he could not hang
on another second, but he kept saying to himself, "You
just got to hang on a little longer."

He managed to get out and on the ground at the edge
of the well and then everything went black. When he came
to, he looked all around. It took him a while to realize
that he had made it to the top and that he was a laying on
the ground by the well and was not still in the bottom of
the well.

By this time the pain was so severe that it was
almost unbearable. He laid there for some time wondering
what to do. He could not catch the horse and hollering
would do no good, for there was no one around for at least
a mile and a half. All of a sudden he heard the morning
train a coming up from Douglas.

Then the thought ran through his head, "That's what
I'll do. I'll crawl to the train track and the next train
that comes by, I can get some help."

Can you imagine crawling a mile and a half on your
hands and knees, not saying anything about a foot that was
a paining? It was a long, hard struggle to the tracks,

This is the well Daddy was a digging when he fell
and broke his ankle. Mamma is in the background
holding Henry. O'Cow is in the foreground and
Junior, her daughter, is in the background. Her
granddaughter is between them. More about them
later.

through ditches and around brush, but he made it there by that afternoon after passing out several times.

When he got to the railroad tracks, he put his red bandana in the middle of the track, hoping that someone on the train would see it and stop the train. Then he crawled to a safe place to wait 'til the next train came by, and that seemed forever. His ankle had swollen to three times it's normal size and was a hurting like the devil.

His heart skipped a beat and a lump came into his throat when he heard a train a coming in the distance. It was a freighter and was a coming along at a good clip in order to make that little hill just before it got to the train station. It did not slow down even a little bit when it came by him. It just passed by as if he was not there.

As the caboose passed by him, the brakeman saw and recognized him and saw that Daddy was in trouble. He went to the end of the caboose and pulled the air on the train, which stopped the train some two hundred yards away. Two men ran back to where Daddy was a laying.

As they approached, one of them said, "What happened, Bert? Are you hurt bad? Can we take you to the hospital?"

He heaved a sigh of "yes" and the two men gently carried him to the caboose.

By this time the head brakeman had walked back to the end of the train to see why the air had been pulled. (They never pull the air to stop the train unless it is an emergency. This lets all of the air out of the train and it stops real fast.)

When he learned what was wrong he hurried back to the head end to tell the engineer. As soon as he reached the engine, the engineer gave two short toots on the whistle. They got a high ball from the rear end and the train started to move again. When the caboose got even with the station, the rear brakeman gave him a stop signal.

The men loaded him into a horse – drawn wagon and they started to the town of Bisbee, some eight miles away, to take him the mining company hospital. The ride to the hospital was not so bad after what he had gone through to this point.

When the men got him in there, they just left him. They knew that he would be there for a long time.

For some reason I could never understand, when the doctor looked at my dad he just shook his head and said, "I'm sorry. We can't help you here."

This angered my dad and he said a few unkind words, got down on his hands and knees and crawled out of that hospital. He was so mad that his foot stopped hurting for a while.

A neighbor came by about that time and gave him a ride home. He hopped into his little tin shack and sat down on the edge of the bed, thanking his neighbor for his kindness and said that he would be alright without a doctor's help.

He said, "A dog will get well from a broken leg and I guess a human being can do the same thing. After all, a man can do what he makes up his mind to do. I made it out of that well and I guess I can make it the rest of the way still better."

From what had happened to him and the way he felt toward the doctor he said, "I don't need any dope to kill the pain. I will grit my teeth and bear it."

The neighbor went outside and cut him a big pile of wood and stacked it by the cook stove and said, "Bert, I'll get you a bucket of water before I go and will be back tomorrow to see how you are."

"That will be fine." he said, "My folks should be here by then."

And then the neighbor drove off. My dad looked down at his foot, which still had the shoe on it and it was swollen over the top of the shoe. Even to look at it made

it hurt worse, but he knew that it had to come off. So he
got out his pocket knife, which was as sharp as a razor,
and went to the painful job of cutting off his shoe.

When this was done, he reached down with both hands
and laid his painful foot and leg on a pillow, then laid
back on the bed and took a deep breath, for he had held
his breath half of the time he was a cutting off that
shoe.

He kept telling himself, "It will stop hurting
pretty soon if I can keep it still."

His ankle healed amazingly fast with his "home"
treatment. It was not long 'til he could get around with
the aid of a pair of crutches, but it was some time before
he could go back to work at the express company, however.

The Train Robbery

Some time later, Daddy hadn't been back to work but a
month or so, he was waiting for the afternoon passenger
train to come in. Looking up the tracks, he saw the train
come to a stop before it got to the train station. This
was very unusual. He knew that there was something wrong.
So he went to see what was the matter.

My dad was always pretty cautious and did not take
many chances and what he saw did not look good. He knew
that the train might be carrying the payroll for the
mining company. It paid the men in gold and it was sent
there from El Paso, Texas.

So instead of going down the track, he slipped around
in back of the mesquite brush 'til he came to where the
train was stopped. He stood there for a minute. Every —
thing looked alright, so he stepped out and went in the
direction of the train. When he was within a few feet of
the engine, the shooting started. He hit the dirt and
laid real still, hoping that no one would see him.

The engineer fell to the ground, mortally wounded. The baggage man jumped out of the baggage car and following him was one of the bandits with a sawed off shot gun.

The baggage man put his hands up in the air and said, "Wait a minute, boys."

But, just at that time, the bandit let him have it in the belly.

He grabbed at his stomach with both hands and said, "Oh my God! You'll have to pay for this throughout eternity!"

And then he fell face down to the ground.

The shooting stopped and here came the other bandits out of the baggage car with a bag of loot. They got on their horses and left as fast as the horses could go in northerly direction.

By the time the sheriff could be notified, they were long gone.

I don't guess they ever saw my dad a laying there in the mesquite bushes. If they had, there would have been more blood shed.

It's been told that the bodies of all five of the bandits were found after they had been dead for a long time. It seems that they got into a fight among themselves and some of them were killed outright and the rest of them were wounded and died a little later at different places over the countryside.

But no one has ever found the loot or the sack it was in. Some of the people around there believe that it was buried and since that time there has been many people a looking for it, including myself, years after the incident happened.

CHAPTER 2

THE BEGINNING OF A NEW FAMILY

Daddy Finds A Wife

My dad was bound and determined to make a go of the homestead and to have a real nice place to truck farm. He was a real good truck farmer, for this was what he did in Texas before he came to Arizona.

He was also a beekeeper and had a few hives of bees. He wanted to combine the two jobs. He thought that he could peddle honey, along with the vegetables, to the miners in Bisbee and make a pretty good living. But this all took money to get started. So he thought if he could sell a portion of his homestead, he could do what he wanted to do. At least, that's what he had in mind. So he decided to sell the forty acres that were south of the railroad tracks for fifteen dollars an acre. It was good land and was fairly flat.

He put an ad in the *American Bee Journal*. That was a little bee magazine that most of the beekeepers subscribed to and it had a nation – wide circulation.

The ad read something like this, "*For sale. Forty acres of good land in good bee country, southeast Arizona, near Bisbee. Write or see Bert Swan, Box 900, Warren, Ariz."*

A month or so went by and he didn't hear a thing from the ad that he had put in the *Bee Journal* 'til one day when a bum got off the train at the Osborn depot.

This bum went up to my dad and said, "Do you know a man around here by the name of Bert Swan?"

My dad was suspicious and very cautious as to why this bum wanted to see Bert Swan. So he questioned him as to what kind of a fellow this Bert Swan was and what the connection he had with him was. The bum still did not identify himself and neither did my dad.

Finally the bum said, "Is this good bee country around here?"

Daddy knew then, he had a nibble on his ad and he replied, "The best in the west, I think. Lots of mesquite and that is a good quality of honey, too."

Then the bum said, "Is there any land for sale around here?"

The thought went through my dad's head, "What would he use for money if there was?"

But he answered, "Down that way about half a mile." One man was as anxious to buy as the other one was to sell, but neither wanted the other to know it and both were a jockeying for the advantage and neither of them was a giving an inch. This went on for some time 'til my dad got the best of the other man and found out that he had ridden a freight train all the way from Milwaukee, Wisconsin to look at his place and that he was not a bum after all. He had the money to buy the property.

My dad moved right in and got the cash for the place and cinched the deal, feeling very victorious.

This seemed to set a pattern for their behavior towards each other for this was the way they treated each other each time they met as long as they knew each other.

Daddy learned that the man's name was George E. Moore

and that he had a big family and a big farm in Wisconsin and that he was very tight with his money. Mr. Moore took the next freight train out of there and went back to get his family.

Daddy didn't hear from them for a long time, 'til one day a freight train set two boxcars off on the siding at Osborn. In them were Mr. Moore and all of his family, all of his cows, bees, chickens, furniture, and all the things he had on his farm back in Wisconsin that he thought he might need in Arizona.

My dad, having the Western hospitality about him, helped them to get their family comfortable as soon as he could, for he knew that riding a boxcar for two thousand miles under these circumstances was hard on the woman and the kids. He shared his place with them until they could get a house built and a well dug and get set up.

It took some time for them to unload all of the stuff from those boxcars and haul it by team to his place. The livestock came first and next was the bees. And this was a job to move bees by horse and wagon, for if the bees got out and stung the horses they might run away and that would be the end of the bees. It wouldn't be too good for the horses, either. So they spent all of one night moving the bees with no mishaps. Daddy didn't say how many colonies of bees Mr. Moore had, but by the way he talked it must have been in the neighborhood of a hundred and fifty or so.

Daddy took the money he got from the place and went truck farming down on the San Pedro River close to a little town by the name of Saint David, hoping to make more money. Then he planned to come back to the homestead and really fix it up.

He left his own bees on the old homestead and would go back from time to time to look after them. That was a long trip in those days. It took him two days to make the trip over and back.

25

George E. Moore and his daughter, Olive, sitting on the Arizona – Mexico border monument.

Olive and a friend sitting on a donkey. Olive is the one on the back end.

He did not make the trip too often, but when he did, he always went over to see the Moores and have dinner or supper, whatever the case would be.

One day, he was up there for supper and when they were all through eating and the dishes were all done, all of the Moore kids (five in all) began to play some games and they invited my dad to join them, which he did.

It was at this party that he discovered that Olive Moore had grown into a beautiful young woman. She had long black hair and freckles all over her face.

The more my dad went to see the Moores, the more Olive and he thought of each other − − and the better care the bees got, but the truck garden was more neglected, to the extent that he had his father, Henry H. Swan, go to Saint David to stay and work in the garden. By this time Grandma Swan had died.

Now Bert and Olive were seeing each other quite often, but there was a big problem. He was thirty − five and she was fifteen, but when people fell in love, I guess that doesn't matter. So they decided to get married and the only way that they could figure it could be done was for them to elope. So they started to make plans as to when they would do it and how they would get rid of her father long enough to do it.

My dad came up with a scheme that he thought would work. He told Mr. Moore that he had some stuff that he wanted to give him at his place down on the river in Saint David and that he should take his wagon down there and he would give it to him.

Daddy told Grandpa Swan what to give Mr. Moore when he came and whenever he started to go home to give him something else and to keep this up as long as he could, even if he had to give him everything on the place and to keep him over night if he could.

Olive was working for one of the neighbors and my dad went by and picked her up. Then they went to town and were married by the Justice of Peace on Oct. 7, 1913.

That evening they went back to her folks house to wait for her father to come home to break the news to him gently so that he might not be too upset. Both of them were scared to death to tell him.

Well, Olive's father got home about ten o'clock that night and as soon as he walked in the door my dad said, "Mr. Moore, Olive and me got married today."

He snorted through his nose and said, "That's a fine how do you do. So that's what this was all about, huh?"

He seemed to be more upset that he had one put over on him than that his daughter was getting married so young.

My father and mother stayed with the Moores that night and the next morning they left for Saint David by horse and buggy to start a new life together.

Their actions also started a feud between the two men that never ended.

This was the first house Daddy and Mamma lived in, in St. David, Arizona.

Mamma shortly before her marriage.

CHAPTER 3

DADDY AND MAMMA'S EARLY MARRIED LIFE

Back To The Old Homestead

Daddy and Mamma stayed in Saint David for a few months and then sold out and built a house on the old homestead. It was in this house that all five of us kids were born. My dad got a job in Bisbee.

It wasn't too long after that my older brother, Henry, was born. In those days very few women went to the hospital to have their babies. Most of them had their babies at home and the doctor went to the house for the delivery.

This worried my dad a lot, so before the baby was due, he hired a woman to stay with my mother so she would not be alone when he could not be there. It would take a long time to get the doctor, especially if it was at night. Daddy kept the horse up and ready to go when the time came. It was a sixteen mile round trip on horse back. It took about two hours, there and back, and sometimes those little babies don't wait that long. That was what he was afraid of. Well, it seems that he had worked extra hard on THE day. He was real tired and went

to bed early. Sometime in the middle of the night he was
awakened by my mother.

She said, "It's time! You'd better get the doctor!"
So he got up and put his clothes on and hitched up old
Buck to the buggy and started out for town to get the
doctor.

From the way he has told it, he was as nervous as any
new father would be. The only difference is, he had some –
thing to do rather than walking up and down the hall in a
hospital.

That poor horse was the one that I feel sorry for.
He had to do double time to town and back.

Well, he got the doctor and was back in time. In
fact, he had to wait several hours before the little one
arrived. When he was born the doctor did what was to be
done and my dad paid him his fee of fifteen dollars and he
went back to town. It was September 26, 1914.

They named the baby Henry Albert after Henry Hunting,
my dad's father and Albert, after himself. He was a cute
little fellow and grew real fast.

It Was My Turn To Be Born

Now let me tell you about when I came to live with
Daddy and Mamma and my big brother, Henry. I followed him
by the space of two years and things were pretty much the
same as when Henry was born. The main difference was that
I started to arrive on the ninth day of September in 1916,
but I was a little on the slow side. At least, it seem so
to my impatient father, enduring mother, and Dr. Fergeson,
who tried to get a few winks of sleep on a secondhand army
cot at the foot of the bed where my mother was a laying.
You see, he would sleep when he was not needed by my
mother.

Well, I got there sometime late the next morning. My

31

dad paid him his usual fifteen dollar fee and he went back
to town. I think that my mother told me that it was about
ten o'clock when I was born and I was hungry enough for it
to be noon, and I hadn't had my breakfast, either. She
said that my favorite thing to do was to eat. I would eat
all of the time if I had a chance. I soon added pounds to
the already ten pounds that I was born with.

My dad named me Walter James, after one of his
cousins that he thought a lot of and hoped that I would
grow up to be like him.

Two years later, my little sister, Hazel Elizabeth,
came along on the second day of September.

By the time I was three I started remembering, and
the first thing I can remember was Henry taking me to the
outhouse in back of the house and lifting me up on the two
holer and wiping me when I was through. He complained
because I would not hold still for him. Then he would
shake me and holler at me and say, "Hold still, you wiggle
stick!"

This was the beginning of the big – brothering I would
get from Henry for the rest of my life.

This is our Grandfather, Henry Hunting Swan
holding Henry.

Mamma with me 'n Henry

me 'n Henry, early 1917

"me 'n Henry"

Me at nine months, June 1917

me 'n Henry. I was about 18 months old and
Henry was 3 1/2 years old.

"me 'n Henry"

Daddy with me 'n Henry in 1918

CHAPTER 4

REMEMBERING EARLY CHILDHOOD

First Snow

The first snow that I remember came a long time 'for
I went to school. I was just a little bitty shaver. I
remember the kind of clothes that me 'n Henry wore. They
were coveralls that were all blue except for the red band
that was around the sleeves and the waistband, which was
about an inch wide. They buttoned down the back and there
was a row of buttons that went straight across the back so
that the seat could drop when I went to the bathroom.

I had a pair of button shoes that were shiny black
and you had to button them with a button hook. When I had
all of this on I felt real dressed up. When I would go to
bed I would fold them up and put them under the bed.

One morning, when I got up and started to put my
clothes on, they were all wet. I went to my mother a
crying and told her that Henry had wet on my clothes
during the night and she should whip him, 'cause every
time I wet myself I got a whipping.

I still remember that she took me in her arms and
said that it had snowed that night and the snow had blown

"me 'n Henry"

Mamma and me 'n Henry making a snowman.

Me 'n Henry with our snowman.

in under the door and got my clothes all wet and that Henry was still asleep.

Mamma went outside and got a big bowl of snow and brought it in the house. She put some sugar and cream on it and we all ate it. And it was real good.

There was so much snow on the ground that we could not go to the outhouse, which was about five hundred feet away, 'til my dad shoveled it away.

When it was a little warmer that day, me 'n Henry went out to play in the snow. It was a lot of fun. We made a snowman and threw snow at each other 'til we were all wet. Then we had to go in the house to warm up and dry off.

That was the most snow we ever saw there. There was about one foot of it. All of the hills were covered white with it and it stayed for a long time. After it had all melted I kept a wishing that it would snow all summer long so that we could have some of that good ice cream again.

Adventure With The Range Boiler

It was back in 1920. We were a living in a two room wood frame house that was heated by a wood cook stove. It was an all purpose stove. It had some pipes in the fire box that water could go through to get it hot and then it would circulate and be stored in back of the stove so that you could have running hot water when ever you wanted it. That is, of course, if there was a fire in the stove or there had been one there sometime that day.

This was the most up to date stove you could get. Montgomery Wards sold them for thirty – five dollars. This was a long time before there was any such a thing as a hot water heater in the house.

Well, this was a good thing if you had running water in the house, but the only kind of running water we had

was the kind you ran to the well with a bucket and got,
then ran back to the house with it. So my mother had my
dad take the tank, or range boiler as they were called,
out so there would be more room in the house.

Well, it laid out there for some time 'til one day as
my dad happened to go by it, out came a white leghorn hen
a cackling at the top of her voice. He bent down and
looked in there and saw that there were some eggs in
there. He started to get them with a stick, but couldn't
reach them. Then he called me.

I was on the back step a petting some little kittens.
I was the littlest kid at home except for my baby sister
and she couldn't walk yet and Henry was too big.

Daddy said, "Walter, crawl in that range boiler and
get the eggs for me. And be careful that you don't break
them 'cause we don't have any eggs in the house now."

I got down and started to crawl in there, but it was
pretty small and I was scared 'cause it was dark in there.
But I started in, anyway. There was just barely room
enough for me, even when I had my arms a way out in front
of me and I had a hard time of crawling in there. My dad
gave me a little help by pushing on my feet.

I finally got to the eggs, and there were three of
them. I started to back out and I found that I couldn't
move an inch 'cause my hands and arms were too far forward
and I had nothing to help me back up. I had the eggs in
both hands and didn't want to break them.

I was getting scared and I started to cry. I thought
that I was going to smother to death and they would have
to bury me in that range boiler. Soon I heard my mother
and I could tell that she was scared, too.

Daddy said, "Don't worry. I'll get him out."

So he went and got a piece of wire that he used for
catching the chickens and tried to hook my britches. But
that didn't work.

Mamma said, "Why don't you pick it up and see if you

43

can bounce him down. Be careful that you don't hurt him."

When he did this, I started to scream even louder. That didn't work, either. The next thing that he tried was nailing two boards together. He put them in there and started to twist them until he managed to catch a hold of my pants. Then he started a pulling.

By now I was really stuck and he had to pull as hard as he could. I was hurting every time I was moved a little and I would holler that much louder. He couldn't tell whether he was a hurting me or I was just scared.

Then, all of a sudden, the boards came loose, tearing my britches, but by now he had pulled me far enough that he could reach me with his hand. He got a hold of my foot and pulled me the rest of the way out.

I got to my feet and ran over to my mother with tears a streaking down my face.

"Look, Mamma! I didn't even break the eggs." I cried.

Henry, 5 yrs; me, 3 yrs; Hazel, 1 yr.

"me 'n Henry"

Hazel, cousin Melba, me, cousin Gene, & Henry

CHAPTER 5

GROWING EXPERIENCES

The Model T

One day Daddy hitched old Buck up to the wagon and he and Mamma went to town. They left me 'n Henry at home to look after our little sister, Hazel. It seemed to me that they were gone for hours and we kept a watching towards the top of the hill for them to get back home. You see, the house was in a little valley and the road towards town had to go up over a hill.

Me 'n Henry had been a watching that hill for some time, when we heard a noise like a motor running, or something a coming. Then a car came into view and when it got closer we could see that Mamma was a driving it. A few minutes later, here come my dad with Buck and the wagon. They had gone to town and got a new car!

It was a Model T touring car with big brass head lights and a big brass radiator with the letters stamped in the front of it that spelled "F O R D". Everyone, in those days, always kept the brass parts shining like a new dollar whether the rest of the car looked like anything or not.

47

The seats were made out of leather stuffed with horse
hair. It had a big black canvas top and there were
celluloid windows that turned a little yellow if they were
left in the sun very long at a time.

The steering wheel was made of wood with four iron
spokes in it with two levers just below it. The one on
the right was the gas and the one on the left was the
spark. If the spark was not pushed all the way up it
would backfire or "kick", as we always used to call it.
There was no self – starter. The only way to get it started
was to crank it. Often, Daddy would crank 'til he was
blue in the face and it still would not start. Then,
again, it would start right off. After he got it to
running he would adjust the spark 'til it sounded about
right and was not a smoking.

Down where his feet could reach them, were three
pedals close together. One was the brake, the middle one
was the reverse, and the other one was low or neutral.
Low was all the way down. Neutral was half the way down.
So when he got ready to go and the engine was still a
running he would push it all the way down on the low pedal
and give it the gas by pulling down on the gas lever and
then let off on the low pedal and we were in business.

We had quite a hill to climb and so Daddy always
tried to get a good run at it, or, in other words, it took
a lot of momentum to make it up the hill. Most of the
time we did, but when we didn't we had to let it roll back
down the hill and start all over again.

It seemed that it took a long time to get to town,
but it was a lot faster than walking. When we would come
upon anybody with a horse and buggy, the courteous thing
to do was to pull over and stop and let them go by before
we moved on because there were a lot more horses and
buggies than there were cars on the road.

If we were to come upon anyone that had a flat tire,
it was an unwritten law that we were to stop and help

This is our Model T parked by the Greenway
School. That is me looking out the back
window. I had to stay in the car because
I had been a naughty boy.

them, even to the extent of loaning them our spare tire, if necessary. That is, if we had one.

That Model T was an important part of our lives from then on. Me 'n Henry were ready to go any time it was.

The First Airplane To Come To Bisbee

There was a lot of excitement around that little town of Bisbee one day when I went to town with my dad in the Model T. There were a lot of people gathered around a talking. We thought that maybe someone had been hung the night before, so my dad inquired and found out that an airplane was a coming to Bisbee to fly.

"Where would it have a place to land?" my dad asked.

"Down at the C & A Copper Company Cemetery south of town." someone answered. "That's the only flat place around here."

Nobody had ever been buried there. They just had set it aside for that purpose, but it was still called the C & A Cemetery.

Some of the men in town took their teams and scrapers and flattened all of the bumps so that it would have a good place to land.

Well, that airplane did not come by air. It was brought in on a railroad flatcar. We found out which day it was a coming in and we all went to the siding to watch all that went on.

It was all taken apart. It was a great big thing with two wings and over – sized bicycle tires and a funny looking place for the chauffer to sit. (That is what pilots were called in those days, there in Bisbee.)

Well, they hauled it to the cemetery with a team of mules on a big flat wagon. It took two days to get it put together and get it ready to fly and we went to see it when it did.

There were a lot of cars there, but there were more
horses and buggies than anything else.

It was about ten in the morning when the plane was
ready to take off. The "chauffer" wore a pair of motor —
cycle goggles and a cowboy's large red bandana around his
face when he got ready to fly.

The way they started the plane was by turning the
propeller. It took them a long time to get it started,
but when they finally did, the dust really flew. It made
an awful roar and started to move ahead and from where I
was, all I could see was a lot of dust.

Others there saw it take off of the ground by about a
foot or so and set back down. He did that a couple of
times and the flight was over.

They took it apart again and loaded it onto the wagon
and took it back to the siding where the flat car was.
And that was the first airplane flight in the town of
Bisbee. I don't remember the exact date, but it was some
where about 1920.

After that, once in a great while we would see a
plane go over the house. When this happened, we were all
made to go into the house for fear that a wrench might
fall out of the plane and hit us on the head.

The Easter Picnic

Mamma had cleared away the supper dishes and said,
"As soon as you boys help me with the dishes we will color
some eggs for Easter. It's tomorrow, you know." And that
was a real fun time for all of us, even better than
Christmas time.

You see, my mother had boiled some beets all
afternoon to get the color for the eggs. It was a lot of
fun to color them even if they were all the same color.
The only variation was the names that she wrote on them

with a birthday candle before they were put in the beet
juice and that would leave them white where the candle
writing was.

Well, I guess she boiled up a dozen or so, but a lot
of them were brown eggs and we didn't color them, just the
white ones.

But that isn't all she did. She spent most of the
day a making a lot of good stuff for a picnic the next
day. You see, we were a going to the river, that is, the
San Pedro River for our picnic. I do believe that my
mother got as big a kick out of it as we did.

That was quite a drive down there. It was some
twenty miles from the house, but that was part of the fun,
a going there in the Model T 'cause it went real fast. We
could get there in about and hour. That is, if we didn't
have any flat tires or stop to help some that did have a
flat.

When morning came we were all excited about going,
but my mother was more interested in getting all of the
picnic stuff in the Model T. Well, it really wasn't *in*
the car proper. It was on the running board. You see,
this Model T we had, only had doors on one side of it and
the other side had a carrier on the running board to carry
stuff that you wanted to haul and it came in right handy,
except when it rained.

We got all of the good stuff loaded up and all we had
to do was wait for the neighbors to come. Well, we waited
'til we were about to give them up, when here they came
over the top of the hill. As soon as they got there we
split up and some went in their car and some came with us.

Me 'n Henry rode with Daddy and the neighbor,
Lawrence, and the picnic stuff. All the other kids rode
in the neighbor's car with their mother, Julia, and Mamma
was driving. Daddy was driving the car we were in and he
took the lead. The women folks followed. We wanted to
beat the women folks there by a little, but we wanted to

keep them in sight, too.

We had been a going for a while when my dad said, "Walter, look in back of us and see if they're a coming."

You see, that was before there were any rear view mirrors.

I looked back and said, "Yep, they're a coming like a bat out of hell and they're making more dust than we are."

Just about that time my dad's hand and my nose had a collision and my nose started to bleed all over the car and on some of the picnic stuff that the neighbors had put in the back seat with us.

Well, my dad pulled the car over and stopped to take care of me. It wasn't too long 'til my mother caught up with us and she came and tried to get the bleeding stopped. I was not hurt, but was just a bleeding a lot.

You know, it was years later before I figured out why my dad had slapped me. And this is the way it was. You see, my dad was not always careful about what kind of language he used when us kids were around and I had picked up a lot from him 'cause I wanted to be just like my dad and this embarrassed him and he had reacted this way.

Well, they finally got me all put back together and we were on our way to the river. We found a sandy spot and the women folks went about a putting out the picnic goodies on a sheet that they had brought for that purpose while the men folks went and hid the colored eggs.

All of us kids were in the Model T a trying not to peek so much that we would get caught by the women folks, but yet enough to know where the eggs were hidden. You see, they went down the river a little ways 'cause the grass was a little shorter there.

As soon as they had hidden all the eggs, they came back to the car and we were given some instructions and a little brother or sister to go with to help them find some eggs, too.

Henry, Hazel, & me a sitting on the running—
board with a friend on an Easter picnic.

Getting the car packed for an Easter picnic.

Well, we all started out a hollering like a bunch of
wild Indians a looking here and there. I knew where a lot
of the eggs were hid, but when I got there they were gone.
We all ran around there for a while and then went back to
the picnic. There were only four eggs found and that was
all. My dad said, "Is that the best that you kids can
do?"

And we all said, "You hid them too good."

So he said, "Come on! Let's all go and see if we can
find the eggs."

Well, he hunted and wasn't having any better luck
than we were.

"I can't figure that out." he said, "I know that I
put one right here."

Just about that time we saw a big black crow a flying
overhead with one of those eggs in his mouth. Now we knew
what had happened to all of those colored eggs. The crows
had beat us to them.

"Well, let's all go back to the car and eat." Daddy
said. But by the time that we got there, the ants were
having a picnic on all of that good stuff we had brought
with us and there was no way that we could share with
them. So we all went home and had some cornbread and
milk. It was not the happiest Easter that I ever had, but
I never forgot it.

Innertube Beach

It was back about 1923 in late July. The summer
rains had started pretty good and the big swimming hole
just south of us by about a mile was full of water. Most
of the folks that lived around there called it "Innertube
Beach". To me, it was a fun place to be in the summer
when it was real hot.

You see, how this got to be such a big place to swim

55

was like this. There was a railroad a moving into this
part of the country. They were laying the railroad bed
and when they would come to the little hills, they would
cut them down with a team of horses and mules and put a
pipe in the gullies to carry off the water when it rained.
We called them "cuts".

Well, I don't know what happened, exactly, but that
railroad was never completed. Most of the work was
already done. All that was needed to make a good swimming
hole was a matter of a few days work with a couple of
teams of mules to fill in the cuts.

I don't remember who it was that did the actual work
on it 'cause I was too little then. All that I know about
it is the fun that everybody had when they were there.

There were cars parked all over the place on the
weekends and everyone took their turn at jumping off the
diving board. But I spent most of my time a gathering up
pollywogs around the edges of the pond. When I got tired
of that I would kick my feet in the water 'til somebody
would growl at me for making the water muddy.

Well, one day when we were down at Innertube Beach,
my mother said to my dad, "Why don't we teach Walter how
to swim a little?"

I was really afraid of the water if it was much over
my knees. Daddy took me out where it was a little deeper,
but I would just freeze my arms around my dad's neck and
that was all the farther they got.

Mamma said, "Why don't you get him an innertube and
fill it with air and then maybe he won't be so scared?"

My dad didn't like this idea very well 'cause this
meant jacking up the Model T and taking off one of the
tires and getting out the tube. But he did it anyway.

Now they had a hard time of keeping me away from the
deep water. As soon as Henry saw how much fun I was a
having, he wanted a tube, too. So we took turns.

If you were to look around at some of the other cars

Some friends and neighbors at Innertube Beach
Mamma is in the middle.

"me 'n Henry"

Mamma and Daddy at Innertube Beach

"me 'n Henry"

Innertube Beach on a Saturday in 1922

59

that were there, you would see that some of them had a
wheel or two jacked up with the tires off, too.

Well, when it was time to go home and we were just
about ready to leave, I thought of my pollywogs that I had
in a tin can and I asked my dad to wait a minute 'til I
could get them. I held them on my lap all the way home so
that all of the water would not spill out going over the
rough road.

My dad was still a grumbling about having to go to
all that work to get me an innertube to play with.

Then Mamma said, "Why don't you get some more
innertubes just for that purpose?" He thought maybe that
might be a good idea and he stopped a grumbling by the
time that we got home.

He went down to the well and got a bucket of fresh
cool water and we all had a big drink.

I put my pollywogs in a big glass pitcher that Mamma
said that I could use and I put them on the middle of the
table so that I could watch them swim around. I watched
them 'til it was time to go to bed.

Daddy blew out the kerosene lamp and we were all
asleep in no time and all was quiet.

Sometime in the middle of the night, I was awakened
by the sound of my dad a gagging and the next thing that I
heard was the sound of glass a breaking in the front yard.

Then I heard him say, "That's the last time that
Walter is going to have pollywogs in this house!"

I finally figured it all out and this was the way it
was. Daddy had gotten up in the middle of the night to
get himself a drink of water and he swallowed some of my
pollywogs. This made him mad and he took the pitcher and
threw it out the front door.

Well, we went to Innertube Beach as often as we
could, but the next time we went, there was a tube for
each one of us kids to play on and when we went home,
Daddy made sure that there were no pollywogs in the car.

Old Buck

It was a Saturday afternoon and we had spent most of the day down at Innertube Beach.

When we got home Mamma got us a little something to eat and as soon as we were through eating Daddy looked over at Mamma and said, "Shall I do it this afternoon?"

You see, he was a talking in a kind of a code that was supposed to be understood by just the two of them and none of us kids were supposed to know what was going on. But we had a pretty good idea what he was going to do.

Well, this is how it was. You see, the old family horse that we had, by the name of Buck, had outlived his usefulness. He was the one that took my dad and mother away when they ran off and got married. He was the one that went after the doctor when me 'n Henry were born. He was the one that went and got the cows a thousand times. And now he had been replaced by a Model T Ford. And this was to be the last day of his life and it made me feel real sad.

You see, what my dad really said to my mother was, "I am going to take old Buck up the 'cessment hole and shoot him this afternoon. I don't want any of the kids a coming along at all."

And this was what his code words meant.

But as soon as I was not being watched, I slipped out of the house and followed him. I stayed back far enough not to be seen, but yet close enough to see what was going to take place.

Daddy led Old Buck up to the edge of the hole so that as soon as he shot him, he would fall into it. He dropped the rope that he had tied around Buck's neck and cocked the rifle. As he raised it and aimed it at the head of old Buck, a lump came into my throat and I started to cry.

This time old Buck did not look at my dad. I think he knew that this was it and that he had reached the end of the trail.

I put my hands over my ears and shut my eyes and waited for it to happen. There was a loud crack from that rifle and I heard a lot of kicking.

As soon as it was all over, daddy went back to the house, but I stayed hidden there for a while before I went to the house 'cause I knew that I was sure to get a spanking if I got caught.

You know, to this day I still feel sad when I think about it. Me 'n Henry would make regular trips up to the old 'cessment hole to see old Buck 'til the coyotes and buzzards had left nothing but the bones. But me 'n Henry still have fond memories of old Buck.

A Christmas Surprise

We had just finished eating breakfast one morning and just before Daddy went to go out in the cold to check his coyote traps, Mamma said to him, "Do you know what day this is?"

He was silent 'cause he figured that he must have done something wrong, or at least she thought he did.

Then she said, "This is the day before Christmas and you haven't gotten the kids anything for Christmas, yet."

You could tell by the way that she said it that she was really upset with him.

Well, he got his coat and hat and left the house before a fuss could get started. Maybe he could think of something.

You see, we were very poor at the time and there was no money at all in the house and he was a hoping that he could catch a few coyotes and sell the furs, but he was not having much luck.

But this morning it had changed a little. When he came back he had two coyotes with him. I had wanted to go

with him but he said that it was too cold and my shoes had
too many holes in them.

   He stretched out the furs and as soon as it warmed up
a little he had thought of a good idea and he said to
Mamma, "I know what we can do. I will take the two boys
to the Bisbee city dump and let them see if they can find
some good stuff to play with."

   Well, she didn't like the idea too well, but it was
better than nothing and this was something that me 'n
Henry always liked to do. So we bundled up and were on
our way in no time.

   Me 'n Henry had a lot of fun. We gathered up a whole
lot of good stuff. At least it was good stuff to us. I
guess I was a natural born junk man. We found some old
Model T parts that we could put together, and maybe, if we
found enough parts we might even be able to put a whole
car together.

   We loaded it all up in the Model T, except for that
which had a lot of grease on it and might get the car
dirty. We had a real treasure here and we could hardly
wait 'til we got home so that we could show it all to our
mother.

   I guess the joy that we had in getting all this good
stuff to play with kind of rubbed off on her a little,
'cause now she wasn't so upset and there was harmony in
the house once again.

   Well, me 'n Henry worked with those car parts trying
to fit them together 'til it got dark. Then we went in
the house and had some cornmeal mush with a little milk
for supper. That was what we had eaten for about a week,
but it still tasted good and we were happy and warm
inside, especially me when Mamma would give me a big hug
and kiss me and tuck me into bed.

   I was 'most always the first one awake in the
morning. It seemed awful light outside for the sun to not
be a shining, yet. So I opened the door to have a look

and it had snowed that night and it was real pretty outside.

As I looked I saw something out there in the yard. It looked just like a Christmas tree covered with snow. I wanted to go outside and see, but I was a little afraid to 'cause it was too cold. So I started a yelling to everybody about what I saw and soon I had everybody in the house awake.

Daddy said to Mamma, "Walter is seeing things again. He sure has a wild imagination."

"Well, put your clothes on and go see what it is, anyway." she said.

We all stood at the door and watched my dad as he went out there. And there, under the snow, was a tree, alright, and there was a present for every one in the family under it.

Daddy brought the tree in the house and we made some decorations out of some colored funnies that we had there and put them on it.

After we had a bowl of cornmeal mush and it had warmed up a little, Daddy and Mamma bundled us all up and we all went outside and played in the snow. They even helped us build a great big snowman. To me it looked about eight feet tall.

That was the best Christmas I ever had and it impressed on my mind, as young as I was, that happiness and joy come to us by doing the best that we can, and we shouldn't worry about what we haven't got.

To this day it is a mystery who put that Christmas tree and the gifts in our front yard. I hope that they had a Merry Christmas, too.

Trapped By A Finger

We were going to town to get a few groceries in the

old Model T and most of the time when I got to go, it was
a fun thing to do. I always sat in the back next to the
window. It was not any fun to sit in the middle 'cause
you couldn't see anything there.

This model of a car was the kind that the top could
be let down when the weather was pretty. There were some
holes that you could put a rope through to hold it down so
that the wind wouldn't get under it and blow it off.

Well, all of the way to town I tried to put my finger
in one of those holes. The hole was a little too small,
but I kept a trying 'til finally I got my finger in there
and I pushed it in as far as I could. When we got to town
I tried to take it out, but it wouldn't come out. My
finger was stuck in that hole!

Mamma stopped the car in front of the P. D. Store and
said, "Walter, do you want to get out?"

I said, "Naw, I'll just stay right here." holding
my other hand over my finger so that she could not see
that I had it stuck.

Well, she was in there a long time and by now that
finger had started a hurting real bad. So I spit on it
and rubbed it a little, but that didn't do any good. Then
I tried to pull on it and that only made it hurt worse.

After a while, Mamma came out to the car with a lot
of good stuff like apples and candy and she said,
"Walter, you can have an apple if you want one."

And I said, "Naw." I was still holding my hand over
the finger. By now it was starting to swell up and I was
getting real scared.

When we got home, everybody grabbed a bag of
groceries and went into the house. When I didn't come in
my mother said, "Walter, you come in this house this
minute or I will come out there and paddle you."

I didn't go in, of course, and here she came after me
with an angry look on her face. She grabbed my hand.
That is, the one that was not stuck and started to pull me

65

out of the car. I let out a holler. When she saw my
finger and how bad it was swollen that anger on her face
turned to a horrified look.

She turned me loose and ran to the house a calling to
my dad. This scared me to death and I started to cry and
pull on my finger as hard as I could, but it didn't do any
good.

Soon Mamma was back with Daddy and between sobs I
could hear her say, "We will have to cut his finger off
to get it out." Then I was **REALLY** scared to death!

My dad took a look at my finger and said, "It's
really stuck! Soap won't do this any good."

He turned to my mother and said, "Go to the house and
get me a piece of string about a foot long and I'll see if
it will work."

Well, he took that string and wrapped it as tight as
he could on my finger and then he pulled on my finger and
at the same time he unwound the string. He repeated this
process several times and it wasn't long 'til he had me
out of that fix I was in. He did not have to tell me not
to put my finger in there again, but he did.

He also said, "Walter, there is always a way to
solve all problems if you keep your head about you."

"me 'n Henry"

Henry's first day of school at the Greenway School in Warren AZ 1920. He is the small boy in the dark suit and hat in the middle.

"me .'n Henry"

Me on my first day of school. 1922

Mamma and Daddy 1922

"me 'n Henry"

Hazel, Henry holding Oliver, and me. 1923

CHAPTER 6

SCHOOL DAYS

The McKinley School

Henry had been going to school for some time before I did. The hardest thing that I ever did was to try to convince my mother that I was big enough to go to school, too. I would measure myself beside her and say that I was big enough now.

And she would say. "This fall you can go to school." And that's all I could get out of her.

Well, that day finally got there and I was all dressed up in knicker bockers (that is knee britches that buckle at the knees and there were long stockings the rest of the way down my legs to my feet.) That is what all of the little boys wore when they were dressed up and I felt real dressed up.

There was one thing that I wanted, though, and that was a lunch box. I kept a fussing about that 'til my dad got a box that an innertube had come in. He knocked all of the talc out and cleaned it up a bit and Mamma put my lunch in it. Then I was ready to go to school.

The name of the school was McKinley. It was on

71

Center Street in Warren. (Warren was the little town next to Bisbee.)

We went up the steps and went in to register. Then the teacher told my mother that there would not be any school 'til the next day. Mamma took me by the hand and we started to go home, but I didn't want to go home.

Mamma said, "What *is* the matter with you, Walter? Come on, let's go home now."

"But I haven't eaten my lunch yet, Mamma." I complained.

"All right, go up and sit on the steps and eat it. Then we'll go home."

And that is what I did. It sure tasted like an innertube, but I ate it, anyway. By the time I got home I sure was sick, and I was sick for the next several days. But by Monday I was alright again and this time I didn't use the innertube box for my lunch.

The first few days a going to school were a lot of fun. There were a lot of kids to play with. That was especially fun for me 'cause we lived so far away from everybody that I didn't have other kids to play with very often.

One day I was a teeter – tottering and when the bell rang, the kid that was on the other end jumped off. The next thing that I knew, I was being carried by a man that I didn't know, toward the school. My back was a hurting like crazy. I laid on the couch at school 'til my dad came and got me.

That night I messed my britches and I didn't tell anyone for fear that I would be in trouble. I went to school the next day that way and I spent most of the day out in the hall on a chair.

My mother smelled me that evening when I got home from school and she got out the washtub and heated some water on the wood stove and gave me a bath even if it wasn't Saturday.

Then she kept me home for the next few days 'til I got to feeling better.

The Sliding Books And The Billy Goat

The McKinley School was built on the side of a hill and one end of it had a set of steps that were thirteen steps tall. They were made of concrete and there was a rough concrete bannister on the outside edge.

It was a fun thing to slide your books down. Well, you see, I would start them a going at the top, then run down the steps and try to catch them before they hit the ground. Sometimes I was fast enough to get them, but most of the time I missed. This is how I entertained myself while waiting for my dad to come to pick me up to take me home after school.

After about three days of this kind of treatment, the book was not readable any more. So the teacher sent a note home telling my dad that he would have to pay for the book I had worn out. He did. Then he took it out of my hide. As bad as it hurt to sit down, I swear that book didn't cost that much!

Well, that stopped the book sliding, so I decided to entertain myself by swinging on the swings. I thought that this was a lot of fun and my books would be readable for a long time. But when I looked up, there was a big billy goat at the corner of the school house.

He had eaten most of *The Little Red Hen* and had started in on *The Three Little Pigs*.

I wanted to rescue them, but all of us kids were scared to death of that billy goat. I didn't know, for a while, which was worse, the goat or my dad. I finally persuaded the goat to go away, but by then all that was left of my book was the covers.

You know, I have always blamed that old billy goat

for the fix I'm in today.

Money In The Ashes

One day I was let off in front of the McKinley School
and I stood there by the Model T for some fifteen minutes
receiving instructions on how I was to act that day and
not to be a bonehead. ("Bonehead" was the word my dad
used a lot to describe someone who didn't think.) I don't
think that it did a lot of good 'cause I went and did what
I wanted to do, anyway.

There weren't any kids there to play with, yet, so I
started for the gully nearby to play down in it. As I
passed by a big pile of ashes that had been dumped out of
the coal furnace that was used for heating the school
building, I saw a whole bunch of money just a laying there
on the ground. It was all silver coins. I started a
picking them up and putting them in my pockets. There was
so much money that there was barely room for it all in my
pockets and it was real heavy.

Well, I carried it around with me all day. Of
course, I gave a lot of it away to some of the other kids
that I was a playing with. I was too young to know how to
count money and know the value of it, so I really didn't
know if I was rich or not, but I felt like I was.

When my dad came to get me after school, he noticed
that my pockets were pretty full. He asked me what I had
and I said that I had some money.

I thought he would be happy, but he had a look of
disappointment on his face and he asked, "Where in the
world did you get that much money?"

And I said, "I found it at school in the ashes."

As soon as we got home he questioned me for an hour
and kept asking the same things over and over again as if
he thought that I was not telling the truth.

The next day, when he took me to school, he went in with me and we went to all of the teachers and asked them if they had lost any money and all of them said that they hadn't and didn't know of anybody who had.

So Daddy looked at me and said, "Walter, come and show me where, exactly, you found all of this money."

He took me by the hand and we both went out there by the pile of ashes.

I pointed my finger at the big pile and said, "Right there!"

He bent over and started a pawing in the ashes and soon found several more coins. As soon as he had found the first one, there was a different expression on his face.

Now I felt better, too. I felt that he finally did believe me, after all.

The Buttons

My Dad was a working on a cement job in Warren. I think that it was up on Black Knob Street. He would take me 'n Henry to school on his way to work. Henry was going to the Greenway School at the time and I was going to the McKinley School. I think I was in the first grade.

Well, on this particular day, my mother didn't have anything to make a lunch out of, so my Dad said, "I'll bring you something to eat from the P. D. Store. If I'm not there by noon, come over to where I'm working and we'll go get you something to eat."

It seemed to me that it was a long way from the McKinley School to where my Dad was working and I was a hoping that he would bring me some lunch. But he didn't. So I started out a walking to where he was working. I walked and walked and walked and I was getting so tired. I thought I would never get there. I was thirsty, too.

And by now, I was getting scared and started to cry. I couldn't find Black Knob Street.

The only thing that made me feel better was to chew on the buttons on my shirt. Finally, I chewed off the first one and I wallered it around in my mouth 'til I swallowed it. Then I started on the next one and the same thing happened to it, too.

It was a getting real late and I was afraid that the sun was a going to go down when right before my eyes was my Mamma and Daddy. They had been looking for me up one street and down the next one 'til they finally found me. I was SO glad to see them! They put me up in the front seat of the Model T between them and we started for home.

By now there wasn't a button left on my shirt.

Daddy looked down at me and said, "What happened to all of the buttons on your shirt, Walter?"

I said, "I ate them all 'cause I was so hungry."

"You What?" my mother said, "Ate them?"

Just that moment the Model T came to a sudden stop and my Dad said, "Walter, get out and start walking home!"

By now, we were about at the Warren Ball Park. I got out and started a walking and they followed in the Model T about ten feet behind.

I was already so tired that I could hardly walk as it was, and hungry on top of that.

Well, this started a fuss between my mother and my father and I could hear her say to him, "He has had enough. Let him ride the rest of the way home."

Well, I had walked almost to the Country Club by now. That was a distance of about a mile, I guess, when the car stopped and I was told to get in and sit down. This time I sat in the back seat all by myself.

I was asleep in no time and I don't remember anything 'til the next morning when I woke up and had started down the path to the little tin outhouse, when Mamma called to me and said, "Walter, here, take this bucket and use it instead. I have to find those buttons 'cause they're hard to come by. I will wash them off and use them again."

You know, it was awful hard to go in that bucket. I don't know whatever happened to all those buttons. All Mamma could ever find was two of them. She washed them off good and sewed them back on my shirt, then she found some different colored ones and sewed them on for the missing ones.

Well, the next day when I got home from school, I had eaten my buttons off again.

When my Dad saw me, all he said was, "Walter, what's happened to you? Have you turned into a billy goat?" 'Cause this time I had eaten some of my shirt, too.

By now Daddy was at his wits end and I thought for sure that he was going to whip me real good.

But he changed his mind and said, "Walter, don't you know any better than that?"

I hung my head and said, "Yes."

"Then if you know better, why don't you do better? Or are you going to be a bonehead the rest of your life?"

A Terrifying Experience

When I was in the second grade, the most important things were recess and lunch time and time to go home.

Well, on this particular day, when it came lunch time, my big brother had eaten his lunch and then he came over to where I was. I hadn't started to eat, yet.

He said, "Walter, can I have your lunch?"

And I said, "Yeah, I'm getting tired of sour cream sandwiches on homemade bread." That was what we'd had every day for so long that to look at sour cream I would get sick at my stomach. So it was no great loss to me for Henry to eat it.

He was just a finishing off the last bite when I saw
that what he was eating wasn't sour cream at all. It was
some good stuff, boiled ham and cheese, and he had eaten
both of my sandwiches and didn't say a word to me about
what was in them. I guess that is the reason the he had
bummed me out of them.

Well, this made me mad and I started to cry and if I
had been a little bigger I would have given him a
whipping, but all I said was, "When I grow up, I'm going
to tell you about this and then you will feel bad."

I knew that it wouldn't do any good to tell Daddy or
Mamma.

Now I was as hungry as a bear, but my lunch was gone.
It wasn't long 'til it was time to go in for the rest of
the afternoon.

My teacher's name was Miss Bloom and she was kind of
fat and was mean, too. I was already hungry and mad and
having to put up with her made the afternoon go awful
slow.

About an hour before it was time to go home, my
mother came and got my brother, Henry. She came into my
room and told me to wait there at the school when it was
out, and that she might be a little late a getting back
and for me to play there until she got back, but to be
sure and not wander off and get lost like I had done once
before.

Boy, that hour sure was long. I would look at the
clock every minute. I guess I couldn't tell time, yet,
but I knew when it was time to go home.

Well, it finally was that time and everybody went
home except for me. I went down in the gully and I was a
playing by myself. I played there for a long time. The
sun was a getting pretty low and I began to get worried.
Mamma still hadn't come to pick me up, yet. I began to
cry. My face was all streaked from the tears a running
down my face. I sure felt neglected.

All of a sudden, there came up out of no where, two of the biggest boys I ever saw. One of them got a hold of me and twisted my arms behind my back. I tried to get loose, but he was too strong. He was a hurting me and I started to holler as loud as I could.

The one that wasn't holding me said, "Go ahead and holler as loud as you want to. There's nobody around here to hear you. We're going to kill you."

And he picked up a big rock about as big as a baseball and was going to hit me over the head with it. He made two passes at me, but didn't hit me. I guess he did it just to scare me and hear me holler.

Then he said, "The next time, I'm going to hit you!" Then I hollered as loud as I could for help, hoping that someone would hear me.

The next thing I heard was someone say, "What in the world are you two big boys doing to him? TURN HIM LOOSE!"

They wasted no time turning me loose and started a running away. I was so upset that all that I could do was run to the man that rescued me and I hugged him around his legs.

He sat down beside me and put his arms around me and this made me feel a lot better. I begged him not to leave me 'til my mother came to get me, but he said that he had to go and catch the streetcar in time to get to work on the afternoon shift at the Campbell Mine Shaft. He said that if they came back to hit them with a rock. This made me feel a lot better.

It wasn't too long 'til Mamma came and picked me up and we went home.

I didn't waste any time in getting myself a slice of bread and honey and a glass of milk.

To this day, neither my father nor my mother ever knew what happened to me that day.

Evelyn

When I was in the second grade there were a lot of
other things that interested me a whole lot more than
learning how to read *The Little Red Hen* and *The Three
Little Pigs*.

There was a big gully that went by, just to the north
of the school a little ways. This was where we all played
a lot. We would take an old railroad spike and dig us out
a road in the side of the bank, about five inches wide.
Then we would use this road for a pretend railroad. We'd
wire a lot of sticks together for the railroad cars.

Well, we were a playing down there one day after
school while we were a waiting for a ride home. There
were several other kids there a waiting with me. There
was only one girl and there were four of us boys. Two of
us were a playing in the gully and the other two were a
sliding down the cement bannister on the school house. It
was about fourteen inches wide and it was pretty high. I
guess it must have been all of ten or twelve feet from the
ground to the top.

About this time I thought I had heard my mother come
for me so I got out of the gully. But it wasn't my
mother. It was one of the other mothers. Instead of
going back to the gully, I stayed by the schoolhouse and
was a watching the boys slide down the bannister, when
Evelyn, the girl, bet Jose, one of the boys, that he
couldn't jump off of the "tippy – top".

Jose said, "I'll jump off the tippy – top if you will
let me see what a little girl looks like, 'cause I don't
have a little sister and I never saw one in my whole
life."

Well, she agreed to it and he climbed up the cement
steps, got on the tip – top and jumped off. He hit the
bottom pretty hard, but it didn't hurt him.

As soon as he dusted himself off, he went over to her

and said, "I am ready to look now."

So she lifted up her dress and showed him and while he was a looking, me 'n that other boy took a look, too. When Jose saw us a looking he got mad and said that if we were a going to look we had to jump, too. So I quit looking 'cause I was afraid to jump that far.

It was not too long after that he was in a fight with the other boy and about that time my mother came.

I sure was glad 'cause I was going to have to fight as soon as he got through with the other boy.

Cactus Stickers

Sometimes there was a lot of yellow mine water in the big gully that ran in it when the flume would over flow. That was a fun thing to play around, throwing rocks in it and watching the water splash. Trying to splash the girls was the most fun of all.

Well, one day, me 'n another kid, by the name of Stanley, were a throwing rocks in this water. Only he was on one side of the gully and I was on the other. We were trying to splash each other.

Boy, that water was sure dirty! It came right out of those copper mines and that made it real yellow.

I had splashed Stanley real good a couple of times and he got me a time or two. So I got this big rock and was a running for the gully and was a going to splash him good, but he jumped back real fast and fell into a prickly pear cactus. He had stickers in him from his heals to his neck.

So I came to his rescue and took him to the teacher and told her of his problem. She was very sympathetic for him. She told me to take him to the boys room and pull out the stickers.

He was sure a funny looking sight. You see, he was a

redhead and he had red freckles all over his body. He took off all of his clothes and laid down on the floor on his belly and I started to pick out the stickers. He sure as the world couldn't sit down at all. Every time that I pulled out one of the bigger ones he would holler and then I would laugh at him. I worked on him most of the afternoon and still didn't get them all.

We finally went back to the classroom and the teacher said, "Stanley, you and Walter go take your seats."

Stanley tried sitting down, but the pain was so bad that he couldn't. The only place that he could get comfortable was on his belly. So the teacher let him lay on the floor the rest of the day 'til school was out.

When I got home that evening and my mother looked at me and my clothes, it was difficult for me to sit down for a while, too.

CHAPTER 7

THE FAMILY GROWS

Sleeping In The Attic

We lived in a two room house. One end of the house was used for the kitchen and the eating area. It was called "the room". The other end was used for the sleeping area and was called "the other room". It was pretty crowded and we needed more room for sleeping us kids.

I didn't know it at the time, but my mother was about to present my Dad with his fourth child. (This was my brother, Oliver.) So to make more room, us kids were moved to the dugout, or the "cellar" as we called it then. That is, me 'n Henry were. They left Hazel in the house. She was only five. I was seven and Henry was nine. Anyway, it was fixed up real nice down there and we really liked our new room.

We had slept there for a couple of nights and on the third night we were sent to bed by ourselves a little after the sun had gone down. We were told not to light the kerosene lamp and to go right straight to bed. It was January, so you know that we went to bed very early that night.

Henry had gotten to bed and I took off my last shoe.
I heard something under the bed, so I picked up my feet
real fast and dropped my shoe. There was no mistake what
it was now. It was a big rattlesnake! Close!! I could
hear him a telling me that he meant business. I jumped up
on the bed and screamed as loud as I could.

Henry was scared, too, and said, "You go get Daddy!"

"You go get him yourself! I'm not a getting off this
bed!" I said.

But Henry didn't want to go get Daddy any more than I
did. So we stayed real quiet and finally he stopped
rattling and finally I got up nerve enough to get off the
bed.

It was very dark now and I couldn't see if that
rattler was under the bed or just where he was, but as
long as I couldn't hear him I figured I was safe. I
wasted no time a getting out of there and to the house.

"Daddy, come quick! There's a rattlesnake in the
cellar under the bed!" I shouted.

"There can't be, Walter. The door has been shut all
the time and that's the only way anything could get in
there. Anyway, you never see rattlesnakes out in
January." He said.

Mamma said, "Maybe you'd better do down there with
him and see what it is. Then he'll be satisfied."

So my Dad took the lantern and the double barrel shot
gun and went out to see what it was. When he saw that
rattlesnake it scared him as much as it did us, I think.
Anyway, he emptied both barrels on that rattlesnake.

We slept on the floor in the house for the rest of
the night.

I could hear my dad and mother a talking about where
they were going to put us boys. It made me feel bad. I
felt like I was in the way and they didn't want me any
more.

The next night I found myself in the Model T. It was about midnight when I woke up. I guess I was cold and it was real dark and I was scared to death. When I went to bed I was in my own bed, but where was I now? I went to the house a crying. Mamma put me in bed with her. She was so warm and soft and it was no time 'til I went to sleep, again.

When I came home from school the next day, I noticed a hole that my Dad had cut in the ceiling and I was wondering what it was for.

I soon found out when Daddy said, "You two boys will sleep in the attic tonight. I've fixed up a nice room for you there."

Well, that was a cozy thought. At least, there are no snakes up there and I would still be in the house.

As soon as supper was over, I was ready to try out my new bedroom. Me 'n Henry went up there by way of a ladder that Daddy had made.

As soon as we got to bed, he took it down and said, "When you want to get down, let me know and I'll put the ladder back up for you."

I felt safe and secure and wanted again. This was going to make a good bedroom.

Some time in the middle of the night I woke up and had to go, real bad! I went over to the hole and the ladder wasn't there and my dad was a snoring so loud that I was sure he couldn't hear me if I called to him for the ladder. And I was sure that I couldn't wait 'til morning. So I crawled over to the far side of the attic and let 'er go.

All of a sudden, the snoring stopped abruptly and there was a sputtering and a growling a coming from my dad. I knew what had happened and I headed for my bed as fast and as quietly as I could.

By the time he got the ladder up there, I had made it to bed with the covers pulled up over my head.

He stuck his head through the hole and said,
"Walter, the next time, before you go to bed, you go to
the toilet first!"

And that was the last time that it was ever
mentioned.

A Rattlesnake Under The Beehive

In the summer, my favorite pastime was to find as
many little cottontail rabbits as I could and put them in
a pen. Sometimes, I would work for hours a digging one
out. And I think that was the biggest worry of my
dad – – that I might get a rattlesnake bite a reaching under
something to catch a cottontail. I was warned, time after
time, not to put my hand where I could not see.

Well, one day, when everyone had gone to town, I went
rabbit hunting. Not that I really did anything with them
when I caught them, but that was all there was to do on
the homestead at the time.

I went a walking down to where the bees were and a
little cottontail jumped up and ran under a bee hive. I
could see his tail as plain as I could see your hand and I
knew that there was no rattlesnake under there. I started
to reach under there and get the rabbit and then I thought
of what my dad had said. So I backed off and looked
longingly under the hive, and headed for the house.

By the time I got there, Daddy had come home from
town and I asked him to help me get the rabbit out from
under the beehive. He was happy to help me for he knew
that I hadn't stuck my hand where I couldn't see and he
praised me for it.

As we came to the beehive that the little cottontail
was under, I said, "See! You can see him from here. If
you will lift on the hive on this side and tip it a
little, I'll grab the rabbit." I was pretty fast and never

missed very many of them.

So he pulled back the hive and tipped it a little and I made a grab for the rabbit. I caught that little cottontail all right, but a great big rattlesnake had him too. When the rattlesnake started to zizzle, I dropped it real quick. But the rattlesnake couldn't bite me 'cause his mouth was full of that little cottontail and that is the only reason that he didn't, I guess.

That rattlesnake was five feet long. Daddy killed it! I still shiver when I think about it, even though it has been years and years since it happened.

Cornbread, Milk, and Honey

It was in the fall and I was on my way home from school, hungry as a bear. As I approached the house I caught the smell of my mother a baking cornbread for supper.

I tried to bum her out of a little sliver to hold me 'til suppertime, but I failed.

All I got was, "You go get in some wood and wait 'til Daddy gets home. Then we'll eat."

As I walked out of the kitchen onto the back porch, I saw a pan of milk a settin' on a table, with nice thick cream on it. You see, that is where we kept things that we wanted to keep cool 'cause we didn't have a refrigerator or even an ice box, for that matter.

The thought went through my mind, "Have a little milk, Walter. I don't mind if I do."

So I took a quick glance around to see if there was anyone a looking, like my little sister, for instance. She was the biggest tattletale you ever saw. There was nobody watching but I knew that I had to work fast. So I buried my face in the middle of that milk, almost up to my ears, and started a drinking.

Boy, that sure tasted good! I managed to get a
little milk along with that thick cream. I drank 'til I
could hold no more and then went outside to get the wood.
Once I was outside, I took out my red bandana and wiped
off my face and tried to conceal all the evidence.

"That will hold me 'til suppertime." I said.

Daddy was a little late a getting home, but he
finally came and we all sat down to the table to eat.
Mamma put the big pan of cornbread on the table and told
Daddy to go out on the back porch and get the milk.

The next thing we heard was him a cussing the cat
that wasn't even in the house. And then we heard the
sound of the milk a being poured into the "pig bucket".

When he came back to the table, Mamma asked, "What
did you do with the milk, Bert?"

"Oh, the blame cat got into it and I dumped it out
for the pigs." he answered.

"Why, Daddy, that cat hasn't been in the house all
day."

"I know better." he said. "Well, put the rest of the
supper on the table on the table and let's go ahead and
eat."

Mamma said. "This is it. Cornbread, milk, and
honey. We don't have any milk now, so it is just
cornbread and honey."

If either one of them had looked over at me they
could have seen what happened to that milk, but I was not
about to volunteer any information as long as that cat had
the blame.

Well, all we ate was cornbread and honey for supper
that night and when supper was over, my big brother went
outside and kicked the cat.

CHAPTER 8

THE SULPHUR SPRINGS VALLEY PERIOD

Daddy's Accident

On April 1, 1924, when my baby sister, Rosa May, was only two weeks old, our family moved from the old homestead (now called Swan's Ranch) down to the Sulphur Springs Valley, some twenty miles away. There were a few of the people who lived there that raised cattle and gardens and some farm crops, but for the most part, they all worked in the copper mines in Bisbee.

My dad rented a place where he thought he could do some truck gardening. The old homestead had proved that he sure couldn't do it there.

We had just got settled down good. Me 'n Henry were a playing over by the pond where there were a lot of weeping willows. It was a real pretty place to play and there was where you could find us any time you wanted to. We always liked to hear the wind blow through the trees.

It was in the spring of the year and the trees had just started to leaf out good and they were real pretty.

Some distance off to the left of us was my mother and my father a washing clothes. Mamma was still not too

strong after my little sister was born and moving so soon
afterwards. That is the reason that Daddy was a helping
her.

You see, he had rigged up a belt to a washing machine
from the same engine that we were using to pump water to
the garden. He had converted an old hand powered washer
so that it would run off a belt powered by the engine.

Well, everything was a going along fine and they were
almost through washing when something happened and quicker
that it takes to tell about, the belt got tangled up.
This engine weighed two or three hundred pounds and some
how my dad wound up under it.

About this time we heard Mamma scream and we came a
running. By the time that we were within a few feet, we
were ordered to get back, A WAY BACK!

The engine was still running so my mother went over
and managed to shut it off.

Then Daddy said, "Go get a two by four and see if
you can pry this thing off my leg."

We were scared and so was my mother. We wanted to
help, but we were told for the second time, to stay back
and we knew that was the best thing for us to do 'cause we
would really get a tanning if we didn't.

But, you know what? My mother didn't even as much as
go to look for a two by four. She just went over and got
a hold of that engine and lifted it off my dad's leg.

You could see that it was broken at the first glance.
Now it was our turn to help. Between Mamma and all of us
kids, we got my dad in the house and into bed before he
had time to pass out.

It was no time 'til his leg was swollen up as big as
a stove pipe. Daddy instructed Mamma to go get the doctor
and that was a long ways to go. So she got the little
baby and left the rest of us at home with Henry in charge
while she was gone.

She always put Henry in charge when she left and this

always made me mad 'cause when this happened he always big
brothered me so much that I couldn't stand it. It was
"Walter do this!" and "Walter do that!" And if the little
kids had a messy diaper, he always made me change it and
wash their behind, and that was the part that I couldn't
stand.

Well, it was pretty late when my mother came home and
shortly after that, the doctor came.

He looked at my dad's leg and said, "Yep, it's broken
in two places. About all I can do for you is to give you
a shot of morphine to ease the pain a little." And all he
succeeded in doing was to make my dad so mad that he
cussed him out and said a lot of unkind things to him.

When Daddy was through talking, the doctor said,
"That's the right spirit, Swan. If you keep up that
fighting spirit, you'll get well. I'll be back to see you
in a day or two and if the swelling has gone down by then
I'll put a splint on it. But in the mean time, lay as
still as you can and it will hurt a lot less that way."

That evening a neighbor by the name of Mr. Stoner,
came over to borrow a plow and as soon as he saw that my
dad was in bed with a broken leg, he was very sympathetic.
He went home and got his homemade radio and brought it
over and hooked it up for my dad. He knew that Daddy
would be there on that bed for quite a while.

The radio was a funny looking thing. It had six
turning knobs on it and if you got them all where they
were supposed to be you could hear music. That was the
first time that I had ever heard a radio.

Well, this was a real blessing to Daddy, but he felt
that he was a taking Mr. Stoner's radio and now he
wouldn't have one for himself.

But Mr. Stoner assured him, "I'll just make myself
another one."

You see, at that time you could get the parts to
build a radio at any Woolsworth store and it wasn't but a

few days 'til he came over with another radio that he had
built to show my dad.

This one was a little different, though. It had a
loud speaker instead of head phones and this was a real
treat. We could all listen at the same time.

To say the least, my dad was well entertained. He
listened almost day and night. And listening to that
radio kept Daddy quiet so his leg could heal.

This act of kindness developed into a life long
friendship for the two of them.

It's amazing how much joy that you can get from being
a good neighbor.

The Fire

My mother had been up most of the night with me
'cause I had an earache and when morning came neither of
us was very cheery, but she still had to drive the school
bus.

Mamma had had to go to work because of Daddy's broken
leg and there wasn't any income with him laid up.

She drove our Model T that we had at that time. Only
about six kids rode the bus and the rest of them rode
burros or horses to school in our part of the country.

Mamma left me home with Daddy. He was still
recuperating from his broken leg. The doctor said that he
would probably be able to get around a little in a week or
two.

Mamma had left without getting him any breakfast, so
he called me in by his bedside and said, "Walter, do you
think that you are big enough to cook me a couple of
eggs?"

You see, I was only about eight at this time and it
was a scary thing for me to light that kerosene stove that
we had then. Sometimes the flames would go up real high

and I was always afraid that it would blow up sometime.

Well, I got it lit without any trouble and turned it up so that the flames were a hitting the bottom of the skillet. I was just about to crack a couple of eggs into it when I noticed a couple of dead flies in the grease. So I went over to the table to get a dish rag to wipe it out with but I couldn't find one.

The skillet, was a getting a little hot by now, so I took it off the fire and began to wipe it out with a piece of paper I found. The part of the paper that I was not using caught on fire and in two seconds it had caught the wall paper on fire and there was a blaze a going up the wall.

My dad smelled the smoke and asked, "Walter, what is the matter?"

I said, "I'll put it out! I'll put it out, Daddy!" And that really brought him out of that bed, broken leg or not.

There was a dish pan full of dirty dishes left to soak over night on the table. With one motion, Daddy took the dishes out of the dishpan and threw the whole pan of water on the fire that was really a going by now.

And that was all it took! It was out and so was my dad. You see, he had hurt his leg all over again and I didn't know what to do. So the only thing that I did was to start to cry.

It wasn't long 'til my mother came in and saw me a crying and Daddy a laying on the floor. Well, she got him revived and back into bed again.

I felt real bad about this for a long time. It took him several weeks more to get on his feet again.

Ever since then I have had a horror of a house fire.

The New Model T

Suppertime seemed to be the time that most of the family business was conducted and this particular night back in 1926, the main subject was centered on Model T's and how old and out of date the one was that we had. So after a while my mother and dad had talked themselves into getting rid of the one that we had and getting a new Model T.

The old one still ran pretty good, but the seats were a little in need of repair. They were made out of leather and were stuffed with horsehair. The hot Arizona sun had made them real brittle. My mother had them covered up with blankets most of the time.

Well, the morning that Mamma and Daddy went to town to get the new car, she left all of the blankets at home and me 'n Henry were left at home to take care of our little sisters and brother.

It wasn't long 'til here they came back home with the new car. We all went out to take a look at it. I was a little disappointed 'cause it was black just like the other car we'd had. I was a hoping that it would be red, but my dad said that black was the only color that cars come in.

But this car was a lot better than the other one that we had. It had a self-starter! And, not only that, it had a battery-powered horn, too!

As I was a sitting up in the front seat, I noticed that there was a mirror up at the top of the windshield and this was something that my dad hadn't seen yet.

As soon as he saw it he said, "Now, that thing has to go. Who ever heard of such a thing as a mirror in a car? If I leave that in there your mother will be a going down the road and will be a looking up there all the time to see if she needs to powder her nose and she'll run smack dab into a horse and buggy or something else." And

94

he wasted no time in taking it down.

Well, after lunch, we all loaded up in the new car and headed for the neighbors to show them the new car.

As soon as we drove in the yard, my dad blew the horn and out came all of the family to see our new car. They looked it over good, but the thing that fascinated them the most was the battery – powered horn.

"Hey, what goes up here?" the neighbor asked.

My dad answered, "Oh, there was a mirror up there, but I took it down. It don't have any place in a car. The only place for something like that is in the house on the dresser."

My dad had a dumb look on his face when he was informed that the mirror was not there for beautifying purposes, but to see if there was someone a coming in back of you when you wanted to make a turn. After this, he was ready to go home.

He hollered to the neighbor for him to "twist 'er tail", or, in other words, take the crank and give it a turn or two to start it up for him, is what he meant.

Just as soon as he had the crank in his hand, my dad stepped on the self – starter and she started right up. And now they were even and they all had a good laugh and we were headed for home.

You know, my dad sure did feel rich with all of those modern gadgets that he had on that car.

The War Game

All me 'n Henry had to do this particular afternoon was to watch our baby sister, Rosa May and change her diaper when she got wet or needed it for other reasons. And for two boys, that was not the most fun thing that we could do.

I said to Henry, "I tell you what! Let's see if we

can get her to go to sleep and then we can play war with our sling shots."

Well, I guess we tried for about an hour before we finally got her to sleep. She was under the cottonwood tree in the back yard where we could watch her.

This war game was that each of us would get a whole bunch of rocks and see how many times we could hit the other one and the one who hit the most times was the winner.

I had first choice of where my fort was to be, so I picked the outhouse. Henry said he would pick the tree just above me. I was sure that I could win 'cause he couldn't carry very many rocks up that tree and I had a whole pile of them beside me.

I waited 'til he got a way up in the tree and he said that he was ready. I said that I was ready, too. So I opened the door of the little tin outhouse just wide enough to get my arm out and I aimed at him.

I didn't even get to shoot at him before he hit me right between the eyes and blood went everywhere, mainly in both of my eyes and I couldn't see a thing.

I started a hollering as loud as I could, "I'm gonna die! I'm gonna die!"

Henry was scared to death. My mother came a running out there and caught me 'cause I was a running around in circles. Then my dad came out there and tried to calm me down.

You see, the reason I was so scared was the day before my dad had butchered a bull calf and I felt just like he looked after my dad had shot him in the head between the eyes. I just knew that this was the end.

After Mamma bathed my face I could see again and I began to think that I would live, after all.

As soon as they took care of my head, my dad got out the razor strap and started after Henry. He got the hardest spanking that I ever saw Daddy give any one of us kids.

As soon as he was through with Henry, my mother said, "It's Walter's turn now."

But all he said was, "Naw, I'm not going to spank Walter. He got it in the head. He's had his punishment already."

After that we got a long lecture on the dangers of playing war games with sling shots.

To this day I still have that scar to remind me how dumb I was and how the little outhouse was a lot better for other things than it was for a fort.

CHAPTER 9

THE FRONTIER SCHOOL

The Flat Tires

I was in the third grade a going to the Frontier
School. It was a little white one – room wood frame
building with a big potbelly stove in the middle of the
room that furnished heat in the wintertime. On one side
of the stove there was a big woodbox for the wood and on
the other there was a table. On this table there was a
big water bucket and a tin dipper. The teacher's desk was
on the far end of the room.

She taught all eight grades, from the first through
the eighth. She was a widow and she had two little girls
who went to school there. One was in the fourth grade and
the other was in the same grade as I was in, which was the
third grade.

There was a recess a going on most of the time for
some of us kids. I think this is the way that the teacher
had of handling such a large bunch of kids.

There was no playground equipment, just burros and
horses that the kids rode to school. This is what the
kids played with during recess mostly.

98

For us littler kids, there was a sand wash that we
called "The Gully", that was about four feet deep. And
that is where we spent most of our time when we weren't in
class.

This particular day, me 'n the teacher's daughter
were a playing in the sand in the wash. It hadn't rained
for a long time and the sand was real dry.

I said, "I'll go to the pump and get a little water
and wet this sand."

She said, "There's no use in doing that. I'll wet
it." And she did!

Then I wouldn't play with her in that kind of wet
sand. So she got mad at me and went and told her mother
something. I never did find out what it was, but whatever
it was it must have been pretty bad 'cause I sure got a
beating.

When I got home that afternoon after school I told my
dad how the teacher had beat me with a piece of stove wood
and how bad I still hurt. But I didn't get a bit of
sympathy out of him. He wouldn't even listen to my side
of the story. He got the razor strap and gave me another
spanking on top of the one that I already had.

Then he said, "Now you can go get the axe and go get
some wood for the stove."

That just added insult to injury as far as I was
concerned and I was real mad. I walked through the garage
with this sharp double – bladed axe in my hand and I saw
some brand new tires that my dad had just gotten from
Sears and Roebuck that day.

The mad was still a running through my veins pretty
heavy yet, so I took a big healthy swing at the left front
tire and laid that tire wide open clear through to the
innertube, but it didn't go flat. Then I got three nails
and put them under the remaining tires. Then I went and
got the wood.

By the time I had cut a wheelbarrow full of wood, I

was all over my mad and I was ready to eat supper.

While we were eating, my dad and mother decided to go for a family fun trip to Bisbee Junction to stay all night with some friends of ours. So we loaded up the Model T with all of the stuff that one would need to stay over night and headed out.

There was a gate some half mile from the house. When my dad stopped there for me to open it he said, "Walter, take a look at that right rear tire and see if it is a little low."

I reported back to him, "Yep, there are three flats. Well, that is, they're darn near flat and there is one that has a big cut on it."

"How in the world could that have happened?" he said. I could have told him, but I was not about to.

Well, we had to pick up all of that stuff out of the car and carry it all the way back to the house. And we didn't get to go to Bisbee Junction.

You know, that was one of the best lessons I ever learned. Don't let your mad tell your mind what to do.

My Revenge

One day the teacher had a gentleman friend come in the middle of the morning to see her. She took him over to the house where she and her two girls lived, some fifty yards to the south of the school building. She left one of the older girls in charge of the kids.

Well, she was gone quite some time and all of the kids were a getting real noisy and so the girl in charge decided to let everybody out for recess. We had a good long one and we had a lot of fun a playing out there.

That is 'til the teacher came back and rang a little hand bell to call us all in.

We went in and took our seats and then she said,

"Walter, come here."

I didn't know why she wanted me to come to her desk, but I got up and went to the front of the room. She reached down in the wood box and came out with a piece of stove wood and she beat the dickens out of me. I was a hurting and wondering what I had done that she was so mad at me.

About this time a couple of the girls in the back of the room were a giggling and this made me mad. I didn't see what was so funny about getting a beating.

Well, I knew that I had better keep my mouth shut when I went home or my dad would give me another beating.

It wasn't 'til the next week that I finally found out what really happened. You see, these two girls had gone over to the teachers house that day she had had her gentleman caller and they had peeked in the window. I guess that the teacher thought it was me and this is why I got the beating.

Well, one morning, the teacher let all of the kids out to play at the same time. We were a playing a game we called "Run Sheepy Run" and while all of the "sheep" were a running, I ran in the school house and slipped a half grown meadow lark in the top drawer of the teacher's desk that I had found while we were a playing. I made sure that nobody saw me and was back out with the rest of the "sheep" in no time.

After about a half hour of this game, we all went in and made a beeline for the table where the water bucket was and we all lined up to get a drink of water before we took our seats and started to study. That is, most of us did. I was keeping a close eye on the teacher and her desk 'cause I didn't want to miss it when she opened that drawer.

Just about then she opened the drawer and here flew out that bird and hit her in the face. She screamed and fainted and fell to the floor. Now is when I started to study real hard.

A couple of girls threw a dipper of water on her and soon she was on her feet again, madder than a wet hen – – and to me she looked like one.

She said, "If I ever find out who did that I will beat him within an inch of his life!"

Of course, nobody knew who put it there and I didn't tell.

Well, the next day I found a horny toad, but this didn't make her faint this time. This was followed with a little green snake. By now she was getting scared to open her desk drawer.

Well, I knew that two wrongs don't make a right, but it sure made me feel a lot better.

Friday afternoon soon came and school was over for another week. The teacher was going to Bisbee for the week end and she would have to be driving against the sun all of the way there. She noticed that her windshield was real dusty and dirty.

Most of the kids had gone home by then, but I was still a waiting for my mother, when the teacher looked over at me and said, "Walter, will you go and wash my windshield for me, please? It's too dirty for me to start out for Bisbee." So I said, "Sure."

I went to the well and got a bucket of water and a rag and started in. I did a bang up good job of it and when I was through I looked down the road and here came my mother for me.

As I started to get in the car with my mother, the teacher hollered at me and said, "Walter, wait a minute. I want to thank you for doing such a good job." And she handed me a dime.

Well, this made me feel real good and from that day on she liked me again. It wasn't long after that that she was able to open her desk drawer without first checking to see what was in there.

The Christmas Play And An Earache

At Christmas time in the Frontier School we'd have a Christmas play. We would take out all of the desks and put them in the yard and then get as many chairs as we could gather up around the neighborhood and put them in the school house for the audience to sit on when we'd have a play.

That was a big time of the year. The kids would practice for weeks to have their parts well memorized and the teacher always seemed to have a part for everybody.

This year the play was about Santa Claus a coming in an airplane instead of his sleigh 'cause he had a broken leg. My big brother was a playing the part of Santa Claus. All there was left for me was the part of Pocahontas and all I had to do was just be there with my tomahawk with a rag tied over my head.

Well, I spent a long time a making that tomahawk to make it look real and I was excited about the whole thing. Henry had his part down pat and he was all set to go.

That evening, we all got in and did all of the chores early. Henry fed the calf while Mamma milked the cow and I fed the pigs.

It was pretty cold that Christmas time and a lot of the times when I would get out in the cold like that I would get an earache. And that was what happened that night! It seemed that the closer it got to the time to go, the more my ear ached.

Mamma warmed up some olive oil and poured it in my ear and then she put a piece of cotton in it and said, "Walter, you go in and go to bed and I will be in after I get Henry all squared away for the play tonight."

But the olive oil didn't help much and my ear was a hurting real bad. In fact, it was hurting so bad that I was crying as I was waiting for Mamma to come in and make it feel better.

Pretty soon I heard the Model T start up in the yard and drive off. I figured that Mamma had stayed home with me and would be in in a minute, so I waited and waited and still Mamma didn't come in. So I got up and went through the house a looking for her and she wasn't anywhere to be found.

Then I really cried. I went back to bed and pulled the covers up over my head to see if that would help, but it didn't. I was going to light the kerosine lamp 'cause it was starting to get dark, but I was afraid to for I might set the house on fire. So I just laid there and cried.

It wasn't long 'til the wind started to blow and that made some of the weirdest sounds when it whistled through the cracks in that old wood frame house.

Then my imagination went wild. I imagined that I could hear the sounds of ghosts a mourning over the people that had died there years before. On top of being scared of the dark and everybody going off and leaving me home alone and me a worrying about who was going to take my part in the Christmas play, I was almost hysterical.

Then a strange thing happened. My ear started to feel a little better and soon I went to sleep.

Morning found me surrounded with a bunch of Christmas candy and a present from my teacher. And this seemed to make things all better again.

CHAPTER 10

MORE LESSONS LEARNED

The Hen And Her Baby Chicks

One day my mother came out to the pond where I was a playing among the weeping willows with a neighbor kid and she said, "Walter, do you see that brown hen over there?"

I answered, "Yes."

"Well, she's a setting somewhere on some eggs and I can't find them. I want you to watch her 'til you find where she's a setting 'cause I don't want the coyotes to eat her and they are liable to some one of these nights. You stay out here 'til you find her."

That sure did spoil our fun that we were a having, so my friend went home and there I was a following this dumb hen around all over the place.

I finally got tired after about thirty minutes of this, so I sat down under a big cottonwood tree to watch her. She soon disappeared under the house and I waited there for about two hours and she still never came out.

My mother came out about that time and said, "Where did she go, Walter?"

"Under the house, right there." I answered, pointing

105

to a hole that wasn't big enough to crawl through.

Well, it seemed like it had been a long time since I saw that hen and I thought that something might have happened to her. So one day, when my mother and dad went to town and left me home alone, I got to studying.

I thought, "What can I do that would be fun that I can't do when they are at home? Hey, I know what! I'll crawl under the house and see if that hen is still there."

I worked and worked 'til I finally got that hole big enough to squeeze through, but when I got in there, it was so dark I couldn't see any thing. So I crawled back out and went in the kitchen and got some matches and tried it again.

I would strike one match and crawl as far as I could on my belly and elbows, for there wasn't much room under there and I almost got stuck a couple of times. I had a hard time a finding that hen.

I think that she was about in the middle. I finally found her a setting on a nest of eggs so I lifted her off. I saw that there was quite a bunch of eggs there and some of them were already starting to hatch, but they weren't all the way out yet. So I decided to help them out. I felt sorry for them all cramped up in those eggs.

So holding a lit match in one hand and with the other hand I picked the shell off of them with a match stick. As fast as I got them out I would put them back under the hen 'til I had helped all of them that were pipped.

Then I started in on the ones that were not pipped. The first one I broke was rotten and I was a running out of matches. So I left the rest of them and crawled back out.

I watched for a couple of days for that hen to cluck all of those chicks out from under the house, but nothing happened. So when no one was a looking I got a handful of matches and went back under the house to see what was the matter.

When I got there and lifted up the hen to see what had happened to all of the little chicks, they were all dead. This made me feel very sad. So I crawled back out again.

I was real puzzled why, with all the help I gave them, they all had to die. So I waited 'til my dad was in a good mood and I asked him about it. I told him what I had done and what had happened.

All he said was, "Well, Walter, there are some things that nobody can do for us no matter how hard they may be. We have to do them for ourselves. Those little chicks didn't get the strength they needed to survive when you helped them out."

The Mule And Fred

While we were a living down on the Felsrud place, my best friend was Fred. We had a lot of fun times together.

One day I said, "Fred, let's go down to where that old dead cow is and see if the buzzards and coyotes have eaten her up yet."

That was about a mile and a half from our house. So off we went on Fred's mule. Everywhere that mule went, she would get as close to the mesquite brush as she could and we would get stuck with the thorns in our legs. We were going real slow, and that was fine with me, until Fred started to lope her. I begged him not to 'cause my bottom was a coming down hard on that bony mule's back, but he kept right on. In fact, he made her go even faster and then we both slid off the back end, saddle and all. Boy! We sure landed hard, all in one pile on the ground.

The mule kicked up her heels and put her head in the air and headed for the house.

Fred looked at me and said, "I guess I forgot to cinch the saddle up."

And I said, "You fool. If you hadn't galloped her we would still be a riding."

We almost got into a fight over that.

"What are we going to do with the saddle?" I asked. It was so heavy that it was all Fred could do to lift it, much less carry it a mile or better.

Fred said, "Walter, you carry it a while and then I'll carry it a while."

Well, this went on for about an hour and then we started to drag it. That was making a mess out of it so we had to stop that. Then we sat down to rest and the longer we rested, the tireder we got.

I said, "I've got a good idea! Let's leave the saddle here and go to the house and catch the mule and then ride her back here and put the saddle on her again."

He said, "Aw, the saddle is no good, anyway. Let's just leave it here. We can ride bareback." That was OK with me. Then he started for his house and I went to mine.

When Fred got home, the mule was in the corral and his dad came out when he saw Fred a walking in, all dusty and tired looking.

"What happened, Fred." his dad asked him.

Fred answered, "Well, the saddle is out there. I don't want it any more."

"Why not?"

"It's too heavy." And then he told him the whole story.

His dad said, "Go to the house and I'll go get the saddle. Where is it?" So he told him.

The next time Fred came over, the saddle was on the mule and it was sure cinched up tight. It was then that Fred told me how his dad had come to his rescue.

We had many fun rides after that together. And you can be sure of one thing. That saddle was always cinched up good and tight.

A Trip To The Farmer's Market

I was always an early riser and one morning after I
got up I went out to the garden to get myself a carrot to
eat. I saw that a cottontail rabbit had gotten inside of
the fence that we had put up there to keep them out. So I
started after him to see if I could catch him. I ran as
fast as I could from one side of the garden to the other.
I noticed that the rabbit was a getting tired. I was,
too, for that matter.

There was a little clump of grass by the corner of
the fence. He came up to it and stopped. I ran up and
grabbed him and he started to squeal, but I hung onto him
and ran to the house with him. I went into the house to
show my dad, who was still asleep, but not for long. He
woke up pretty fast when he heard that rabbit a squealing.

"Look at what I caught! A good cottontail! I caught
him with my bare hands!" I exclaimed.

Daddy said, "Take him out and kill him and we'll
take him to market today."

That was a place that all of the farmers took their
vegetables to sell to the public in an open air sort of
shed. I was a hoping that I could go to market with him.

Most of the time I had to stay home, but this time he
said, "Walter, go wash your feet and if you get them
clean enough, you can go to town with me this time."

I had gone barefooted all summer and they were sure
hard to get clean, but I scrubbed on them 'til they
started to bleed on top and then I dried them off and went
to see if they passed inspection, for I knew that there
was only one chance. I had to get them clean the first
time or that was all.

Well, they passed inspection and I got to go.

At the market, every person that came by, I was a
hoping that they would buy my rabbit.

A man walked up to my dad and put out his hand and

said, "I am Governor Hunt. Let me shake this little boy's hand, too."

It didn't thrill me much. I didn't really know what a governor was. If he had of bought my cottontail it would have thrilled me a lot more.

But the next man that came by, bought it for twenty – five cents. Now I was rich! I went and bought myself a pair of tennis shoes. That is what they cost at that time. Man! It sure felt good to be able to run without stopping to pick out the stickers!

The next morning, I went to the garden to see if there were any more rabbits in there, and there was. I took out after it. I thought that I could run right up on it and catch it without any trouble with these new tennis shoes on, but this time the rabbit found a hole in the fence and he ran off into the mesquite brush. I went to the house a bawling my head off.

My dad came running out and asked, "What is the matter with you?"

I told him and he said, "Why didn't you holler and I would have come out and shot him with the gun?"

So the next morning I found another one and I started a hollering. And here came my dad, barefooted and in his long handles, with the gun and he shot the rabbit.

This went on every morning for some time and we'd take them to the market and sell them.

So Daddy bought a box of shells and put them in the garage in the cupboard.

One day, before going to market, we were going out to shoot some rabbits. Daddy went to the garage to get the shells and they were gone. He asked me if I knew where they were and I said that I thought two boys who had come from town had cut them open and put all of the stuff that was in them on an ant hill and lit a match to them.

This made my dad real mad, but I was the one that got the spanking.

110

My Dad's Illness

We had just finished eating supper, when my dad said,
"Well, as soon as the dishes are done we'll go over and
see the new place that I bought." So we all got in and
got the dishes done in a hurry.

We had been renting a place we called the Felsrud
place. I don't know why it was called that. I guess
'cause some people who had lived there before had that
name. Well, anyway, we had our own place now.

We all piled into the Model T. (Some of the time we
called it the Tin Lizzy.) It didn't take us long to get
there. It was only a couple of miles from where we lived.

It was five acres and the Frontier Road ran right in
front of it. There was a little tin shack on it and a
half – dug well on it that had a little water in it, but not
enough to do any good.

Well, my dad had paid cash for it and he said that
was a lot better than paying rent all of the time. It
wasn't long 'til we were a making preparations to move
over there. While we were moving, we lived in that little
tin shack. It didn't even have a floor in it. We used
the dish water after we did the dishes, to sprinkle down
the floor to keep the dust down.

Daddy and Mamma spent a lot of time tearing down the
house that we were born in down on the old homestead and
bringing it to the new place. They were figuring on
putting it up there and making the well deeper and
planting a garden. Oh, they had a lot of things that they
were going to do.

In the meantime, my mother was driving the school bus
for the Frontier School. Well, it was not a bus as such.
It was just the Model T that we had at that time. All she
did was pick up some six or eight kids and take them to
school. It paid a little money and that is what we lived
on while all of this moving was a going on.

111

Well, this particular morning, my mother had started
out to get all of the kids to take them to school, but she
was having a hard time a starting the Model T and she ran
down the battery. This was the Model T that had the
self – starter on it.

Mamma called for Daddy to come and crank it with the
crank that stuck out in front under the radiator. It was
always there just in case something went wrong with the
self – starter.

When Daddy started to crank it up, he ran a piece of
rusty bailing wire that he had used to tie the license
plate on with 'cause it had fallen off the previous day,
into his chin.

Nobody paid any attention to it 'til about three or
four days later when his chin started to swell up and
start a hurting him. My dad was not much to complain
about pain. You see, he had just gotten over a broken leg
and was still a limping a little when this happened.

His chin kept a getting worse real fast. Pretty soon
he was down in bed with it and my mother had to call the
doctor. That is, I should say, she called on the
neighbors to go and get the doctor from Bisbee for her.

He was the same doctor that had patched up Daddy's
broken leg and had delivered the last baby in the family.
His name was Dr. Brannen.

Well, when he got there, he looked Daddy over and
said, "It looks to me as if you have blood poison and
you're in pretty bad shape. There's not a whole lot that
I can do for you. Stay in bed and put hot packs on it. You
should get better in a few days."

But he didnt! In fact, that night we were all woke
up by him a running out in the yard a screaming with the
pain 'til my mother finally got him settled down.

Then he would get out of bed and have a rolling fit
on the floor 'cause he was a hurting so bad.

And this went on for a day or two. About all my

mother could do was take care of him. She got Mr. Stoner, one of the neighbors, to drive the kids to school for her.

All of us kids were getting real hungry and some of us were a crying we were so hungry. So Mamma sent me to one of the neighbors with a note. I didn't know what it said, but I did bring back with me, a ten pound lard bucket of hot soup and it sure did taste good.

We all had to stay outside all of the time so that we would not bother Daddy.

Mamma sent for the doctor again and we were not allowed to be any where close to hear what he had to say.

After he left, Mamma called to all of us kids and told us that Daddy was real sick and we had to stay out of the house 'til he got better.

Well, by now, the friends that we had in Bisbee Junction had heard about it and one of them came to see my dad. When he drove up in our yard he always let out an Indian war whoop and he did it this time, too. He walked in the house with his cowboy hat on. This displeased my dad. You see, he always taught us that it was not polite to wear your hat in the house.

Then the neighbor talked in such a loud voice that we could hear him from clear outside where we were.

He said, "Bert, what are you a doing in that bed? You need to be out there a building on that house and a getting a decent place for your family to live."

This made my dad so mad that he tried to get out of bed so he could whip him, but he couldn't. You see, my dad had already given up and was sinking fast 'til this happened.

But this was his turning point. Daddy started getting better from then on. There is one thing that I did learn from that. No matter how bad a situation gets, don't ever give up. Just try that much harder.

O'Cow, The Family Cow

As far back as I can remember there was always a lot of good rich, cold, sweet milk for us to drink any time that we wanted it. And there was good homemade bread or cornbread and honey to go with it. There were many times that there was nothing else to eat but that. It was not too easy to go to the store and get a bottle of milk and a loaf of bread. Only rich people did that and we were a far way from being what you could call rich.

Let me tell you a little about our family milk cow. Well, you see, my dad had bought her from my grandad on my mother's side of the family.

Grandad had brought her from Wisconsin in a railroad freight boxcar with all the rest of his stuff and his family.

She was about three years old when Daddy bought her. That was about the time that my dad and mother got married and before there were any of us kids. She was a giving milk by the time that Henry got here.

My dad always kept her, even though he had other cows. She was referred to as the "old cow". And that was her name. Oh, of course, we shortened it down a little and called her "O' Cow" most of the time.

She was the boss of all the other cows. She had sharp long horns and she knew how to use them. Why, she was even boss over Old Buck, the family horse.

I was always kind of scared of her. I stayed out of her way. Daddy and Mamma did all of the milking of her. I think that she was a little hard to milk.

The day that my little sister was born, she had a calf and it didn't have any tail. Daddy carried it into the house for my mother to see.

I can't remember how many calves she had, but it was a lot of them and most of them were bull calves. She had one heifer that I can remember, though, and we named her

114

"Junior". We milked her for a long time, too, but she wasn't nearly as good of a cow as her mother was.

One day I was kept home from school with a little sore throat. I was not really sick, that is, not bad enough to have to stay in bed and that is one thing that I hated to do worse than anything. That was the worst part about being sick.

We were a living down in the Sulphur Springs Valley at that time and still had some cows at the old homestead. We would go down there from time to time to see after them and this was one of the times that we were a going there.

My mother had just gotten back from taking all of the kids to school and she was a talking to my dad. Well, there was some talk as to whether I was to go with him or stay at home with my little sister and brother. When it was all talked out, I wound up getting to go with Daddy down to the old homestead to see about the cows.

Well, we took the old Model T truck and left Mamma the other car.

This old truck had a small bed on the back and no top. We had made it out of that first Model T that Daddy and Mamma had bought. Two boxes that dynamite came in (we called them Apache powder boxes), were used for seats. When you went around a corner you had to watch it or the boxes would slide out from under you. But it was a fun thing to ride in, anyway.

Well, after an hour and a half we got there. We went down by the cement well and there was a big Holstein heifer having a calf. My dad helped her for about an hour and I checked out the rest of the cows.

We were about ready to leave and I said to my dad. "Did you see O'Cow around anywhere?"

Well, he looked around for a little while 'til he found her under the shade of a mesquite tree asleep. When we left and started for the truck, she woke up and followed us.

Daddy cranked up the old Model T, then he rubbed his
chin with his hand and said, "Walter, do you think that
O'Cow would ride in that truck all the way to the valley?"

Well, to me there sure looked like there wasn't
enough room for her. Besides, we didn't have any rope,
either.

Then my dad said, "I'm going to see what she will
do. Maybe we can take her with us."

So he backed the old Model T up to a ditch bank and
took O'Cow by the horns and said to her, "Get up there!"

She got right in the back of the truck and her head
stuck over the boxes where we were a sitting. There were
no sides on the truck and she could have stepped off if
she moved around any at all and there was no rope on her.

I don't know what made her stay there unless it was
my dad a telling her to stand still and she understood
him.

Well, we were under way in a little while and I just
knew that she was not going to stand still for an hour and
a half. But she did! That is how long it took us to go
some twenty miles 'cause of the old rutted dirt roads.

O'Cow was about fifteen years old at the time and I
think that she was really enjoying it 'cause she was a
chewing her cud all the way home. And cow slobbers were a
coming out both sides of her mouth and every time she
turned her head, those slobbers went down my neck and they
were cold and slick. I tried to dodge them the best I
could and stay on that powder box, too.

Well, we got home without the slightest bit of
trouble and as soon as the truck stopped in the yard, I
made a beeline for the house to wash the cow slobbers off
the back of my neck while Daddy unloaded O'Cow.

One day, my mother had started to fix breakfast (and
a lot of the time that was hot milk and toast).

Well, she had made the toast and was a heating up the
milk on the old wood cook stove when she said to my dad,

"Look at this milk, Bert. Is there something wrong with it?"

Daddy looked at it, then said, "Yes, there is. Dump it out!"

And every time after that when she tried to use the milk, it was the same way.

"She's just no good any more." my dad said one day. Well, we kept O'Cow for a long time 'til one day I heard my dad a talking to my mother about where they were going to get the money to pay the taxes.

"The only way that I can see is to sell O' Cow and Junior. We might get enough out of them to pay up the taxes." my dad said.

I watched Mamma and Daddy load them up and I thought to myself that it just ain't fair to have to go that way after being with the family for over twenty years.

CHAPTER 11

BISBEE JUNCTION

The Hobo

By now my dad had recovered from his illness to the point that he could get around pretty well and do a little work. The family was being moved once again.

This time it was to a rented house right next to the Southern Pacific Railroad tracks at Bisbee Junction. Well, it was not really a house. It was an old saloon that was not in use any more. We rented it for five dollars a month while my dad rebuilt the house that he had torn down and hauled to Sulphur Springs Valley. He had intended to rebuild it there in the valley, but things just hadn't worked out for us there 'cause of Daddy's illness.

This was a slow process 'cause he didn't feel real good and could only work just a few hours and then he had to rest the rest of the day.

The landlady lived real close by and came over quite often, too often to suit my mother, sometimes. Well, this particular morning, there was a knock on the door and Daddy and Mamma were still in bed. I was up, but that was all.

Instead of having me answer the door, Mamma hollered out, "Come in!" thinking that it was the landlady. But instead, it was a hobo and he was the dirtiest smelling one I believe that I ever saw.

He walked right in and over to the bed where Daddy and Mamma were and it like to scared my mother out of her wits. My dad did not waste any time a getting out of that bed and helping that hobo outside.

Oh, he was nice enough to him, but my dad didn't want him to get any of his lice all over the house. As it was, Daddy deloused the house after he fed the hobo some breakfast.

I don't know how my dad fed every hobo that came along when there was scarcely enough for us, but he always managed some how. I guess it works on the principle of the more you share with others the more you have.

Two Half Dollars

One afternoon, me 'n Henry were out in the back a boxing with some gloves that somebody had given my dad and we were really a getting after it. I was so determined to whip Henry that I didn't notice the passenger train that was stopped there.

There was a man a sitting on the back end of the train on the little back porch of the observation car. He was watching us. Just as the train was a pulling out, he hollered at us and I looked up in time to see two half – dollars a coming at us. Boy, they sure looked big to us! But by the time we knew what was really going on, the train was too far down the track for us to thank him for them.

That was as much money as you could get if you worked hard all day. We felt like we were RICH!

After that, every time a passenger train came in, me 'n Henry would put on the boxing gloves and put on a fight, hoping that another half – dollar would come flying our way. But all we got was skinned up noses. So after a few times we stopped boxing.

My dad took that money and went to town and bought some groceries with it so we could share our fortune with the rest of our family.

Burned Taters

While Daddy was rebuilding our house we had left all of the cows over at the old homestead. That meant there was a trip over there every day, or sometimes, twice a day to do the chores and it was time to go over there again. Mamma wanted to go so I was left at home to watch the supper that she had started a cooking on the stove. It was a wood cook stove and you had to keep a putting wood in it to keep the supper a cooking.

All I had to do was to stir the potatoes and see that the rabbit didn't burn and set the table. You see, once in a while we would get a rabbit and then we would eat pretty good. As soon as they got back we would eat. At this time, that was all there was to eat 'til we got some money or got some more rabbits out of the lumber pile where they liked to hide.

The last thing that my mother said to me was, "Walter, don't let the taters burn and behave yourself."

Well, they hadn't any more than gotten out of sight 'til the neighbor boy came over and wanted to play.

I said, "Wait 'til I put some more wood in the stove and I'll be out."

Well, I didn't think any more about that supper 'til I saw Daddy and Mamma a coming down the road. Then I looked towards the house and saw smoke a coming out the

windows that were open. I ran into the house and the
rabbit and the taters were on fire on top of the stove.

The neighbor kid went home in a hurry 'cause he knew
what was about to happen as soon as my dad got there.

Daddy put out the fire and fanned the smoke out of
the house, and boy, did it smell bad! It stayed that way
for a long time.

To say the least, we didn't eat that evening and was
everybody mad at me! I got a whipping with the razor
strap and got sent to bed.

After I had stopped crying, my dad came into where I
was and sat down on the edge of the bed and said,
"Walter, you bonehead, the next time that you have work to
do, don't mix playing with it."

And do you know, I never let that happen to me again.

The Cake And The Crochet Hook

This particular Saturday afternoon, we all loaded up
in the Model T and were about ready to go to the
homestead, when my dad looked over at my mother and said,
"Do you think that we had better leave someone here at
home 'cause there has been a lot of hobos pass through
here lately and there is no way to lock up the house?"

When they both looked at me, I knew that I was the
one that had to stay home and I started to complain and
feel sorry for myself.

My mother seemed to have an answer for everything, so
she said, "Walter, you can make a cake if you want to,
but don't eat it all. Save some of it for our supper.
And don't eat too much of the batter. It's liable to make
you sick."

Well, this sort of eased the pain of having to stay
home all by myself and I began to dream about the good
taste of that cake I was a going to make.

121

The first thing that I did was to check the wood box to see if there was enough wood to bake a cake 'cause if there wasn't enough I'd have to go get some and this would take all of the fun out of it. But it looked as if there was enough wood if I was careful. So I started in.

I got out all of the stuff that I was going to use, and began to put it together. I put the flour, sugar, baking powder, and salt in a bowl. Then I added eggs, milk, and lard. I would beat a while, then lick the spoon a while. It was tasting better every lick.

Soon I had all of it beat together and I dipped the spoon in real deep to get my last big taste. As I smacked my lips, I thought, "There is something a missing. What did I forget?"

Then I thought of it and it was the vanilla. I had missed it 'cause my mother kept it hid high in the cupboard 'cause my little brother would get it and drink the whole bottle of it if he could.

Well, I hunted for it a long time 'til I found it clear at the top in the cupboard and I had to reach as far as I could to get it. I didn't any more than get it in my hand when I slipped and fell.

On my way down I bumped into the cupboard door that had a lot of junk in a sort of a little door shelf. Among other things, there was a crochet hook a sticking out and it made contact with my rear end and it went all the way in. That is, all except about an inch of it that was a sticking through my overalls.

That really hurt and I was a letting the world know about it. I was a hollering and a screaming. Then I started to holler for help.

Pretty soon, Mr. Crist, who lived just across the tracks from us, heard me and came a running over to see what all the noise was about.

I was embarrassed to tell him what was the matter with me 'til he looked down and saw that crochet hook a sticking out of my back side.

He reached down and pulled it out. He finally persuaded me to drop my overalls so that he could see how bad it was.

I said, "How bad is it? Do you think it will leave a scar?"

I knew that he wanted to laugh, but he held it 'til one day when our paths crossed some forty years later. Then we both had a good laugh together about it. It didn't leave a scar!

CHAPTER 12

BACK ON THE OLD HOMESTEAD

The Cow In The Mud

After living in Bisbee Junction for several months while Daddy was putting our house back together, we moved again. This time it was back to the old homestead.

One day me 'n Henry had been playing with the neighbor kids and it was time for them to go home. We were wanting something to do that was a little fun but that there wasn't too much work to it 'cause we were a little tired from playing most of the morning.

I said, "I know, Henry. Let's go down to the puddle hole and see if we can find some pollywogs. There should be some there by now. It's been a week since we had a gully washer." (That is what we called it when it rained enough to make the water run down the gullies.)

So I went over and got a couple of my mother's Mason jars. This was not to her liking, but she didn't stop me. So off we went to the puddle hole. It was some half mile from the house.

This was an all purpose spot. You see, the cows watered there and we went swimming there, that is, when

124

the water was not too muddy and the water had not turned green on top. Sometimes the mud was real deep. In fact it would get knee deep if you would stand still for a while.

Well, as me 'n Henry approached the puddle hole, we saw a cow there stuck in the mud. She was not one of ours, but was a stray that wanted a drink and she had broken through the fence to get to the water.

She was real skinny and by the looks of things, she had been there for some time. She tried to get out, but was too weak and would probably have died right there before too long if we hadn't come along.

Well, we tried to help her, but we were just too little. So we went to the house and got our dad. He got the well rope so that he could tie it around her horns to see if we could get her out.

You see, we didn't have a horse at this time or we would have got him to help us get her out. We were going to use the old Model T, but the ground was too rough and we could not get close enough to do any good. So we all decided to do what we could to try to get her out of the mud.

Daddy said, "I'll go in and put the rope around her horns and as soon as I do, you two boys come in and tail her up and see if we can get her on her feet. When we do, you boys come and help me pull on her head. Then, if she starts to walk by herself, you two boys head for the fence and get on the other side of it as fast as you can 'cause sometimes they will come after you and get you if they can."

Well, Daddy got the rope on her horns and gave us the signal and in we went and grabbed her tail and started to lift up as hard as we could, but we weren't getting anywhere.

Then Daddy said, "Boys, wait 'til she wants to try to get up. Then you help her by lifting up on her tail."

125

So we waited there a while 'til she tried to get up.
Then we started a lifting on her tail and she got on her
feet and before we could get around to where my dad was,
she started to walk.

He said, "Steady her by holding on to her tail and
see what happens."

This was working and she was making progress and
there was just a few steps to go 'til she would be on hard
ground.

Then we got the order to get to the fence as fast as
we could. And it was a good thing, 'cause here she came
after us. She didn't see my dad, I guess, but saw us and
almost got us before we could get under the fence. Then
she fell down, she was so weak.

Daddy went up and took the rope off her horns and got
on the same side of the fence with us. We stood there and
watched that cow for some time 'til she got up enough
strength to get up by herself. When she did, she just
walked off and started eating grass.

Then my dad said, "Boys, remember what you just saw.
I can't explain it, but it is so. When you help a cow out
she will try to hurt you and this is the same way it is
with some people. You help them out of a hole and they
will turn on you, too, if you give them half a chance. I
can't explain that either."

Ants, Fire, and Burns

Just south of us there lived a family that we liked
to go visit a lot 'cause they had the same number of kids
as we did and they were about the same ages as we were.
It was always a fun time when we got together. We always
hated to stop playing when it was time to go home. Some –
times they would come over to play with us.

When my mother said, "Come on, let's all go to

Lawrence and Julia's it didn't take us long to all pile in
the old Model T.

They had a Model T about the same as the one that we
had and the men folks would talk about the cars while the
women folks would talk about kids and having babies, and
all of us kids would be playing. If it wasn't cops and
robbers, it was hide and seek or some other fun game.

This particular day we were a playing hide and seek
when our game was interrupted by a call from both of our
mothers. So we all went to see what they wanted.

Well, it seems that they had started to make some
cookies for all of us kids and when they went to get the
sugar they found that the ants were eating it. Our
mothers wanted us to follow the ant trail to the nest then
get some kerosene and put it on the nest.

We had a lot of fun a following that ant trail. It
went every which way, but we finally found the nest. One
of the bigger neighbor boys went to get the kerosene
'cause he knew where his dad kept it. (You see, that is
what all of us used for our lanterns in those days.)

He couldn't find any kerosene, but he came back with
a tin cup full of gas and poured it on the ants. That is,
about half of it, and he set the cup down on the ground.

We were all gathered around the ant's nest a watching
the ants curl up and die and we were a laughing and
giggling and having a good time when one of the little
kids thought it would be funny if he struck a match to the
gas and watch all of us jump back. And we all did!

This was not so funny. We darn near got our hair on
fire.

At this moment the cup of gas caught on fire and was
a flaming way up there. We all didn't know what to do.
We wanted to put it out but didn't know how. While we
were a talking about how was the best way to put it out,
one of the younger kids came up from behind me and gave it
a healthy kick. Before we knew it, that cup of gas and

fire went all over one of the little boys.

He let out a scream and started to run. I took after him and caught him and me 'n Henry started a beating on the flames with our hands, trying desperately to put them out.

In the meantime my little sister, Hazel, was a screaming at the top of her voice. She always was the loudest and best screamer you ever saw.

My mother heard her from inside the house and she said to Julia, "I guess I am going to have to go out there and spank Hazel. She is always a screaming."

As soon as she went out, she saw what was happening and between the three of us, we finally got the fire put out, but the little boy was burned real bad.

Mamma carried him to the house and was met by his mother at the door. She was horrified when she saw her little boy. His hair was all gone and his face was burned, but the worst part that was burned was his right arm and his leg.

Well, they laid him on the bed and took off all of his clothes and tried to make him comfortable while the men folks went for the doctor.

That little boy was sick for a long time. It's strange how fun can turn into tragedy so quick.

Taking Off Honey

It was the last part of May, a kind of pretty time of the year in the southern part of Cochise County. There wasn't much we had to do. This particular day, Mamma and Daddy had gone to town. This was a trip they made once a week and they had left me alone. They would be gone for a couple of hours.

This wasn't time enough, really, to do what I had in mind. Besides, I had to finish baking the bread that my

mother had started. That meant staying there at the house
to keep putting wood in the stove to keep the oven the
right temperature 'til it was done.

Then I was free to do anything that I wanted to,
namely, to eat about half a loaf or so of bread. We
always had a lot of good butter and honey and milk to go
along with it.

I took the bread out of the oven and put it on the
table and covered it up with a dish towel.

Then I had an idea. "Hey! I know what!", I said,
"Instead of eating the old granulated honey, I'll just
g'over to the bees and get some of that good fresh
mesquite honey. There sure ought to be some on the bees
by now and that would sure taste good. Mmmm, some fresh
honey on fresh bread and butter, what could be better?"

I had helped my dad take off honey a few times and
pretty well knew what to do. So I got the bee smoker.
(That is a thing that you put a fired up gunny sack in and
work the bellows and make smoke come out.) I wasn't real
sure why this was necessary, but I was a doing what my dad
did when he took honey off the bees.

He had a hood that he had made out of a piece of fly
screen that fit over his head and the bottom part was made
out of cloth that fit around his shoulders.

Well, I got all of these things together and started
out for the bees that were some two hundred yards or so
away from the house. There were some thirty–five hives in
the bee yard. The wind was a blowing a little. My dad
always said that this made the bees a little mean.

I was kind of scared for this was the first time that
I ever tried to take any honey off the bees by myself.

I had the smoker a going good and the bee net was
over my head and I was ready to start. I opened the lid
and gave the bees a lot of smoke. I pried the frames
apart with the hive tool 'til I found the frame of honey
that I wanted.

So far I hadn't gotten stung. I closed up the hive and started for the house with my frame of honey.

Now, what was I going to do with all of those bees on the frame. I couldn't remember how my dad did this part. You see, I was only about ten years old at this time. I tried blowing them off, but that didn't work. So I took a handful of grass and brushed them off and this worked pretty good. That got most of them. Ten or fifteen bees wouldn't hurt much.

I put the smoker down outside and took the honey in the house, cut it out of the frame and put it on a plate. That is, most of it, what didn't leak over the sides and get on the table.

Well, I had me a real feast with bread, butter and comb honey and a big glass of milk.

Then I looked at the clock and remembered that I had better go feed the chickens and gather the eggs before Mamma and Daddy got home. And then I remembered that I was supposed to clean out the chicken house, too.

I was so busy a doing that, that I hadn't noticed Mamma and Daddy come home. Then I could hear my mother was mad about something and I was not too sure if it was safe to go into the house or not, but I started for the house, anyway.

My dad was taking the groceries in the house and he looked up and saw me.

He said, "Walter, I see you got some honey off the bees and I see you left the door to the house open and I see that the house is full of bees and your mother is quite mad at you."

"But, Daddy," I said, "There's really not that many bees. Only ten or so the last time I was in the house."

"Well, there's a whole lot more than that now."

"Where did they come from?" I asked.

"Well, Walter, you see, the bees are robbing the honey that you took off and when bees do that they are

very mean and your mother has gotten stung and that is why
she is mad."

Well, I got out of that pretty light. All I got was
a lot of instructions on how to keep bees. And the best
thing of it all was that now I had a desire to be a bee
keeper, which has been with me 'til this day.

Learning To Milk

It was a way past time for Daddy and Mamma to come
home from town and the family cow was out in the back yard
a bawling and wanting for someone to come and milk her and
give her something to eat.

Me 'n Henry had been left home with the little kids
to take care of and it was way past suppertime. I cooked
some fried potatoes and fed everybody and they were pretty
happy then. All that was left undone was milking that
bawling cow and I didn't know how to milk and neither did
Henry.

So we talked it over and we decided that I was to try
to milk the cow. So we set up a plan on how we could do
it and this is the way it went.

Henry went and got down the old number two wash tub
that was a hanging on the ocotillo fence. (It was the one
that we all took a bath in and washed clothes in, too.)
He put it out in the back yard and went out to the shed
and got some bran and put it in the tub so while she was
eating she would stand still so I could milk her.

Well, I got the milk bucket and got down on my knees
and started to milk. I was too scared to sit down 'cause
if she kicked she might get me. I put the bucket on the
ground and started in. At first there was no milk a
coming out, then I finally got it started, but I was
having a hard time of hitting the bucket. I think as much
went on the ground as went into the bucket.

"me 'n Henry"

Finally, I had about an inch of milk in the bottom of
the bucket when she had eaten up all of the bran, so she
started to walk away.

Henry ran and got some more feed and said to me,
"Walter, that's all of the bran there is so you had better
get busy and get her milked this time."

But my hands and wrists were getting tired and I
could hardly get any milk at all and the feed was all but
gone.

We kept a looking up the road for Daddy and Mamma to
come home.

I was about halfway through when the cow ran out of
feed again. So I picked up the bucket and stood there
trying to think of what would be the next best thing to do
when my little sister said, "Walter, why don't you feed
her some flour? That will take her a long time to eat and
then you can milk her."

So she went into the house and got a quart of flour
and put it in the wash tub and I started to milk again.

Well, I milked 'til I was through, or I should say,
'til the cow was tired of me a messing with her.

I didn't get all of the milk, but I got most of it,
anyway, and I took it into the house and strained it with
a dish – towel and put the pan of milk in a pan of cool
water to cool it a little. At least, we would have milk
for breakfast.

Well, my folks still didn't come home, so me 'n Henry
put all of the little kids to bed and were just about to
go to bed ourselves when in came Daddy and Mamma.

It had been dark for about an hour or so by then and
the first thing my dad said was, "Walter, go and get the
coal oil lantern and light it and go with me to see if we
can find the cow. I've still got to milk her."

When I told him that me 'n Henry had milked the cow
already, I don't believe that I ever saw him any happier
than he was then, and he said, "How in the world did you

do it?" But we weren't as anxious to tell him as he was to know.

I said, "I think that you will have to use flour in the morning 'cause we used up all of the bran."

Well, from that day on, I was the one that had the job of milking the cow.

The Iceman

There was an ice plant about where the Lavendar Pit is now in Bisbee. That was always a fun place to go, especially around a hot summer day. It was always cool there and I would watch the iceman back his one – horse ice wagon to the plant to get a load of ice.

All of the horses were black and the wagons were covered with a canvas that hung down in the back. There was a place in front for the driver to sit and drive the horse.

I still remember the sound of the horses hooves a going up and down the streets and the melodic chant of the iceman calling out, "Iceman! Iiiicemaaan!" And the echo would answer back off the canyon wall.

That is about all Bisbee is. Canyons! Some places are so steep that you would wonder how they got the stuff up there to build a house with. The streets seemed to me to be almost straight up with such narrow switchbacks that I used to wonder how in the world horses pulling wagons could get up them.

Pretty soon a housewife would come out on the porch and wave a dish – towel and holler, "You – hoo! You – hoo!"

And then you would hear something like this, "How many pounds, lady?"

And she would answer back from the top of the canyon in Brewery Gulch, "Fifty pounds!"

The only way to get up there was to climb a set of

cement steps about a block long and almost straight up and down.

Well, the iceman would take out his ice pick and chop off a block for her and start up there with it on his back, with a happy smile on his face. When he reached the top he was a little out of wind, but that was all in the day's work. He received his pay, which was five cents. (Ice was the same price at the top of the hill as it was at the bottom and that was ten cents for a hundred pounds, five cents for fifty and three cents for twenty – five.)

The iceman was always the most popular man in town with all of the boys and girls 'cause he always gave them the little chips of ice to eat.

As soon as he had sold all of the ice he had in his wagon, back to the ice plant he would go for more.

And this was the daily life of the iceman.

The Balky Horse

Me 'n Henry were a coming to the house after we had gotten a mason jar full of pollywogs out of the gully that had a little water in it, when we saw a cowboy ride up on a horse.

He stopped to talk to my dad and, of course, we were always interested and stopped to listen to what they were a saying. And this is the way the conversation went.

"That is sure a pretty roan gelding you have down there in the pasture. Is he yours?" the cowboy asked.

My dad answered, "He is, but he's no good. He is pretty and you have said it all."

"What is the matter with him?"

"Well, he is balky and as soon as you get him saddled up, all he will do is just stand there. He's not mean or kicky or anything like that, but just no good!"

"What will you take for him?"

Well, my dad scratched his head and kicked a few rocks around on the ground 'cause this took my dad off guard and he was not prepared to do any horse trading. But yet he wanted to sell the horse and get what he could out of it and yet not take advantage of the other fellow.

I think my dad goofed this time 'cause that cowboy took the offer the first go around and the money changed hands in a few seconds. They shook hands on the deal and the cowboy said, "I'll be back in a day or two to get him."

I think that this cowboy saw qualities in that horse that my dad could never bring to the surface and was looking forward to the chance to try to bring them out.

Well, he was back at about ten the next morning in a horse – drawn buggy along with another man. He had a saddle in the back of the buggy with all the rest of the stuff that you need to ride a horse. He unloaded it in the front yard and the horse and buggy were driven off over the hill.

Of course, me 'n Henry were hanging around just to see what was going to take place.

My dad looked at us boys and said, "He is pretty sure that he can get that horse a going, isn't he?"

Well, we all watched him go up to the horse and lead him to the house and put the saddle and bridle on him. Then he got up in the saddle and we could see the horse plant all four feet solid on the ground getting ready to balk. I guess you could say that he was a balking right then.

This cowboy just sat there and nobody was a saying anything, when all of a sudden he started a talking.

"Let me tell you what happened the other day down at the river at Hereford." And this is the way he told it.

"You see, we were a crossing some two hundred Mexican steers across the line at the dipping vats at Palominas. I had five Mexicans a helping me and we were driving them

up the river to Hereford where there's a corral and a
loading chute where we could load them into the cattle
cars. They were a going to an outfit in California.

"Well, when we had gotten there we put them all in
the corral, but there were no cattle cars there on the
siding. So I went to the station and asked the agent
where the cars were and he told me that there was some
delay and didn't know when they would be there.

"So I went back to the corrals where the steers were
and told the other cowboys to let them out 'cause there
was no feed there for them and it was no telling when they
would get there. The steers could not go too long without
any feed. That was open range country there and the grass
was belly deep to a long legged horse. All we had to do
was to sort of herd them to see that they would stay
fairly close together.

"I gave those Mexican cowboys instructions and said I
was going to the little store there in Hereford to get a
little grub and would be back in a little while.

"While I was gone, I ran into some friends of mine
that I used to know in west Texas and we got to talking.

"Well, any how, when I got back there it was about two
in the afternoon by sun time and I found the five drunkest
Mexicans you'd ever want to see. It seems that they had
brought with them across the border, a gallon of that
Mexican tequilla. They were so drunk I don't believe they
could tell the difference between a horse and a cow.

"I looked up the track and I saw a switch engine a
pushing a cut of cattle cars and I knew that they were for
these steers. It was up to me to get them all back into
the corral and get them into the cattle cars that
afternoon. I didn't have time to go get more help. So
you know what I did?

"Well, back and forth I went and around here and
there 'til I got them all a moving in the right direction.
Pretty soon one of them went into the corral, and then

136

another, and it wasn't long 'til they were all in and it
was a matter of just plain work a getting them into the
cattle cars."

By now, the horse that cowboy was a sitting on in
the front yard was all but asleep. Without any warning
that he was ready to go, that cowboy spurred that horse
and he jumped about ten feet and was off on a dead gallop
before he had time to think about it.

And that was the last we saw of him as he went over
the hill.

As me 'n Henry were a walking to the house with my
dad he said, "You know, boys, horses are not too much
different than men. They all have a lot of hidden
qualities that will surface if they are approached in the
right way."

CHAPTER 13

THE AIRPORT

Me 'n Henry Working At The Airport

Back in 1928, just south of Warren by about four miles, there was a tractor a working for some time a clearing off a large area of mesquite brush. I was curious about what was going on. So one day, when I was a coming home from school I stopped and talked to the tractor driver and he told me that it was going to be an airport when it was finished.

While I was at it, I asked him for the wood that he was a pushing up and he said, "Sure. Help Yourself."

So every afternoon after school, me 'n Henry would take the Model T truck and haul a load of wood or two home. That was a lot easier than what we had been a doing to get wood for the cook – stove.

Well, we got a great big stack of it after a while. Boy, we really felt rich! Now we could have more time to play and do what we wanted to.

One day we saw an airplane come in and land there. We were only about a half mile or so to the east of the airport and every plane that came in for landing had to go over our place and that was real exciting to us.

You see, that was just before the big depression
which followed in about a year or two. There was a lot of
money in that little mining town and the Scenic Airways
out of Phoenix would come down there every weekend and for
$2.50 would give people rides over the city of Bisbee and
the surrounding area.

One day we were over there a watching them, when one
of the pilots called me over and asked me if I lived over
the hill from there and I told him that I did. Then he
gave me a dollar and asked me it I would go home and get
him some breakfast. It seemed to me more like lunchtime,
but I ran all the way home and told Mamma about the man
and gave her the dollar.

She smiled and fixed him up a big plate of food. I
was going to take it back to him, but she said, "I'll
drive you over in the car."

When he saw me, he came over to where I was in the
car and that made me feel big and important. I handed him
the lunch Mamma had fixed. When he had finished eating he
asked me my name. I told him and he said that his was
Charlie and that sometime he would give me and Mamma a
free ride in the airplane.

It was a two seater biplane. The model was called a
Husky Junior. It was a kind of a plane that they gave
flying lessons in. It had controls in the back seat,
also, but they were removed while they were flying the
people over the city.

That evening at the supper table, we were all talking
about the happenings of the day and my dad said, "Walter,
why don't you and Henry go over in the morning and see if
you can get a job?"

That sounded like a good idea to me. I could hardly
wait 'til I had finished my breakfast the next day 'til we
went over there.

Charlie hadn't gotten there, yet, but we waited

around 'til he showed up and when he did I was so scared I had a hard time asking him about the job. But Henry was with me and that gave me a little more courage.

He said, "Sure, that sounds like a good idea. How much do you want per day?"

I said, "How about twenty – five cents a day for me 'n Henry?"

"Well, boys, that's a deal! The only thing is that I need you more at night to keep an eye on things around here than I do through the day." So we talked it over with our dad and it was agreeable with him.

There wasn't much of a place to stay. All that there was to sleep in was a small tent and one of us had to sleep outside, but it was summertime and it wasn't bad. That is, except when it started to rain. Then we had to both get inside of the tent.

I remember one night after we had gone to sleep. Way in the middle of the night it started to lightning and thundering and it woke me up. I started to drag my bed in the tent and somewhere between me and the tent was a big rattlesnake a warning me not to come any closer.

I hollered to Henry to turn on the flashlight. He was the only one that had one, but I couldn't get him to hear me. So I dropped my covers and grabbed my pillow and threw it at him and hollered at the same time and this time I woke him up.

I said, "There's a big rattlesnake out here and I want to get in the tent before it starts to rain!"

So he shined the light all over, but we didn't see any snake and he said that I was just a hearing things.

Well, I got all of my covers and put them inside the tent, scooted Henry over and I laid down next to him on the ground. You see, I was still pretty scared. I was sure that snake was going to come and get in bed with me.

The next morning when we got up, we found the snake. He was all coiled up in the corner of the tent. He wasn't

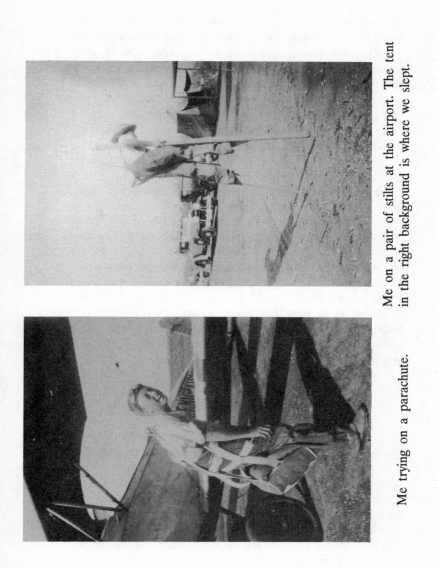

Me on a pair of stilts at the airport. The tent in the right background is where we slept.

Me trying on a parachute.

141

too big, about four feet long, but that was big enough for me! We eased him out of the tent and then killed him.

Charlie usually got there a little after sun up and we went home then. I told my dad about the rattlesnake after we had eaten breakfast. Boy, he was ready for us to quit our jobs right then, but my mother said, "Why don't you get a couple of cots for them to sleep on?"

Well, this was a pretty good arrangement. I felt pretty safe as long as I was up off the ground.

A few days later I got permission to stay all day over at the airport because I thought I might be able to get a ride in the plane if I was handy and in the right place at the right time. And it worked!

That was the greatest thrill in my whole life, when we started to leave the ground. We flew over the house and started for the city of Bisbee. We were getting higher all of the time and the higher we got the more scared I got 'til pretty soon I couldn't look at the ground. If I did I would get real sick and I didn't want to throw up in Charlie's plane. I was sure glad to get back on the ground again when we landed.

It was a long time before I had the desire to go up in the air again.

The Mile High Aerial Club

It wasn't long after that, that they started to give flying lessons there. There was a group of businessmen who got together and formed a club. I think they called themselves "The Mile High Aerial Club", and they were all a taking lessons at the same time. I guess they got a special rate or something. Anyhow, there was someone a training every morning. I think it was that they had to practice with a teacher for so many hours before they could get their solo flights.

I think it was a man by the name of Stewart who was the first one to solo. On this particular morning that he was going to solo, I looked at him and he sure looked scared to me. I was sure glad that I wasn't a going up with him!

That was when you had to start the planes by pulling down on the propellers. Well, he got the plane all warmed up and we were all a standing there watching him take off. I heaved a sigh of relief when he got it in the air.

Charlie looked at me and said, "That is the easiest part of it all. It is when you start to land that you can get into trouble."

Well, Stewart flew around for a while, then he came in for a landing. Charlie saw that he was not going to make it and ran out there and waved him back in the air again.

Then he went around another time. He came in a little better this time. It still wasn't the best, but Charlie didn't wave him back up this time.

Well, he didn't set her down soon enough and the end of the runway came up on him too fast and he didn't have enough speed to take off again. So he ran her out and ground looped.

He got skinned up a little and jimmied up the plane a little, too.

Charlie and his partner worked on the plane for about a week. I don't know what all they did to it, but I do know that they took off the bottom wing and worked on it and then put it back on again.

My Blunder

By the time they got the plane all fixed up, it got kind of dirty. Charlie told me to go clean out the cockpit, front and back.

Well, there was a seat that would accommodate a parachute that the pilot would just sit on. If he wasn't wearing one, there was a cushion that would fit in its place, about the same size that the parachute was. It had two snaps on it, one in front and the other in the back, that held it in place.

I took both of the cushions out to clean the cockpit. I put the back one back in and left out the front one because Charlie was going to take her up and give her a test flight. He was going to wear a parachute, just in case something happened, like the wing coming off that he had just fixed, so he could bail out if he needed to.

Charlie said, "In the morning, I'll take her up and see if she is safe to put back in use again."

Well, he got there about daylight and did all of the preliminary things that he had to do to get ready. By the time the sun was up by about an hour, he was a taking off.

He took her up about 5000 feet or so then he put her through the paces. Then he put her into a dive and he was a coming down and down a lot farther than I thought he should. Then he rolled her over on her back and I saw the back cushion fall out!

Then I knew just what I had done. I had not fastened the seat in back down good and it got lodged between the front of the seat and the control stick used by the student pilots. When he had made the dive, he couldn't pull her out. He managed to turn the plane upside down so the cushion would fall out and get out of his way 'cause he knew what had happened. Everybody else that was a watching him thought he was a doing some fancy stunting like they had never seen before.

I didn't know what to do. I was scared and felt very bad all at the same time and I knew that I was in for it when he landed and that was a coming up real fast. As soon as he stopped the plane, I was there ready to take my punishment.

I don't know how many times he had said, "Walter, be sure that you fasten them seats in good."

His eye caught mine just as he got out of the plane and all he said was, "Walter, you and Henry go and see if you can find that cushion."

He was so white and still a shaking, I do think that if he would have said any more to me then, he would have killed me.

We didn't waste any time a getting out of there. We had that Model T truck a heading off in the direction of that cushion in no time, and, believe me, I stayed away from there the rest of the day.

We never did find that cushion. As far as I know it is still out there in the brush somewhere. I looked for it many times after that, but never found it.

Playing Golf And Chewing Tobacco

Well, by the next morning, things were pretty much back to normal around there and he had started giving flying lessons again to some of the other men in the club.

One particular man was a golf instructor at the golf course some three miles to the north. His name was Chuck and he had gotten everybody at the airport a knocking those little golf balls around and I inherited the job of going out and picking them up.

He would bring out a big water bucket full of them and there would be as many as five or six men lined up a hitting them at one time. Then they would wait 'til I had gathered them all up and start all over again.

I think Chuck sort of took a liken' to me. He bought me a pair of golfing shoes and a pair of knee length pants they called knicker bockers and heavy sox that came to the knees. Boy, I thought I looked sharp! But the fact of the matter was, they were all too big for me by about

"me 'n Henry"

Me in my new golf clothes.

Me getting ready to hit the ball.

three sizes. But the best part of it all was that he made me feel good. I was important and a big shot. I wanted to be like him.

One day when nobody was around I decided to see if I could chew tobacco and spit as far as Chuck did. There was no chewing tobacco, as such, around there and all I could find was a half – smoked cigar that somebody threw away.

Well, I cut off both ends of it and chewed it up 'til I got a big mouth full and I tried to spit just like he did. I hadn't spit more than a time or two 'til I started a getting sick. So I spit it all out and washed my mouth out with a little water.

By now, I was real sick, so sick that I had a hard time of standing up straight and the ground started to move all over the place.

Just then, my dad came. I knew I was in trouble if he found out what I had done.

He looked at me and said, "What is the matter with you, Walter?"

I had to tell him, "Well, it is this way. I wanted to see if I could spit tobacco juice as far as Chuck does and I found out that I couldn't. All I did was to get real good and sick and I'm still sick."

Daddy was pretty mad and said, "You had better quit and come home with me, if you can't behave yourself any better than that."

So we went home and he made me drink a lot of milk, so much that I couldn't hold any more. Then I was really sick. I went out in the back yard and heaved 'til I thought I was going to pass out. Then in a little while, I started to feeling a whole lot better.

By morning my dad had changed his mind and I went back to work and all was forgotten and forgiven.

"me 'n Henry"

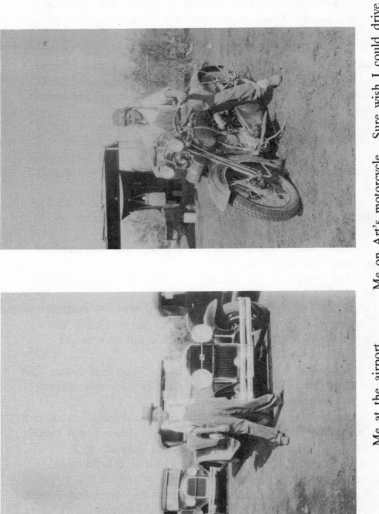

Me at the airport.   Me on Art's motorcycle.   Sure wish I could drive it.

Me 'n Henry when we worked at the airport. The
Model T we used on the old homestead is in the
background. That's our little sister you see on
the left.

A Robbery

Sometime later, I guess it was a couple of weeks or so, we were sleeping at the airport all night, when a way in the middle of the night, Charlie woke us both up and wanted to know where the gun was. You see, he had a 22 rifle that he did target practice with from time to time. He kept it in the tent under some junk he had there. I didn't know what he wanted with it in the middle of the night so I asked him. He said that he had been robbed and was going to get them. He found the gun, all right, but the shells were all gone.

He asked, "Where are all of the shells, Walter?"

Well, Walter knew, but this was not the time to say. I sure didn't want to tell him that I had shot all of them at rabbits and tin cans. So he left the gun there and went back to where his car was and tried to get it started, but the robbers had fixed it so it wouldn't start.

You see, this is what happened. Charlie had gone to Naco on the Mexican side of the line and was a dancing and having a lot of fun and he got acquainted with this girl and decided to take her over to the airport to watch the moon come up.

Well, this was fine, but this girl had a couple of boy friends that needed some money. So they followed them over to the airport where they were parked and robbed him, then took the girl with them. I think that it was a put up job. He lost $80 and all of his rings in the deal.

So from then on, he did his dancing on this side of the line and made sure that they were American girls.

Chewing Gum

One day, Charlie said to me, "Walter, I'm going to

Douglas tomorrow. Do you want to go with me?"

I said, "Sure!"

So the next day I put on my good golfing outfit and was ready to go.

When I got to the airport, Charlie said, "Get over there by the plane. I want to take your picture."

He gave me one of them some days later and I still have it to this day.

Well, going over to Douglas in the airplane was fine. I didn't get sick a bit, and coming back was fine, too, 'til he started to chasing buzzards. Then I got real sick. I was sure glad when we landed and I got my feet on solid ground again.

Things were pretty quiet around there for some time 'til one day my friend, Chuck, brought me some chewing gum in a bag. I thought it was mighty nice of him 'cause I sure liked gum.

Well, I would chew up a bunch and as soon as the sweet was gone, I got some more. It was not too long after that that I started feeling a little sick, then I started getting cramps. Then Chuck started a laughing at me. I couldn't see any thing that was very funny about having the bellyache.

He laughed and said, "Walter, you're going to have to go pretty soon. Those were Feenamints that you were a chewing."

I didn't know what a Feenamint was. This was a good time for my dad to show up and he did. As soon as he saw what was a going on he gave Chuck a good cussing, then he told me to get in the car and we went home. He didn't wait long enough for me to get my pay that I had a coming.

And that was the end of my job at the airport, much to my disappointment.

CHAPTER 14

THE GREENWAY SCHOOL

Poems, Hygiene, And English

Summer vacation was over and it was time to start to school again. This year, 1928, I was bound and determined to do a little better in school and not be the dumbest kid in the class. I was the biggest and the oldest in my class.

Well, first off the bat, the English teacher gave the class an assignment to write a poem. I was never very good at poetry, either writing it or memorizing it, and it bothered me all day. Here I had something, already, that I couldn't handle and I wanted so much to do a good job in school.

Well, that evening when I got home, as soon as I ate supper and did the chores and the supper dishes were done, I lit the kerosene lamp and put it in the middle of the table and I started to write my poem.

"I want to be a farmer and join that happy band,
   With hay seed in my hair and callouses on my hands."

And that was all the further I could get. I sat there at the table just a thinking and a thinking until it

152

got real late.

I was keeping Daddy and Mamma from sleeping, 'til finally my dad said, "Walter, go to bed so we can go to sleep and I'll have a poem in the morning for you."

I was tired and he didn't have to tell me the second time. It was no time 'til I was asleep.

When morning time came, I was usually up before anyone else was, but this morning, Daddy was awake and up, already.

He said, "Walter, get yourself a pencil and a piece of paper and I'll tell you your poem."

And this is how it went.

"I bought a little tree for fifteen cents.
I planted it in the back yard close to the fence.
When it gets big, higher than I can reach
It will have fruit on it, maybe a peach."

Well, I handed it in to the teacher and when I got back my paper there was an "F" on it. Written in big red letters it said, "Walter, you did not do this yourself. Stay in after school and write the sentence one hundred times, 'I will not cheat in English.'"

This was very discouraging and I was about to stop even trying to study any more at all.

That afternoon, I was in Miss Blackwoods class and we were a studying Hygiene. Or, I should have said, the class was a studying Hygiene. I was a looking out the window at some horses that were eating grass some two hundred yards away.

The teacher had told me to get to studying two or three times 'til I got tired of her a telling me the same thing so many times. Then I said that I didn't need to study 'cause I was already smart.

This made her so mad that her chin started a wiggling. She didn't have much of a one, anyhow.

Then she said, "All of you close your books and we are going to have a test."

Pointing her finger at me, she said, "Walter, if you don't make a passing grade you will have to stay in after school for a month."

I came back with the remark that that was fine with me and we started in with the test. About half of the questions were true and false ones and the rest were the answer kind.

Well, when it was all over, the papers were gathered up and I was the only one that got a 100% correct. And all that Miss Blackwood did was to bury her face in her hands and have herself a good cry.

She stayed mad at me the rest of the school year, but I didn't care. I didn't like her either, so we were even.

My Letter To Kansas

One afternoon we were studying English and what we were a studying was the proper way to write a letter. The whole class was to write a letter to an English class in Kansas somewhere and tell about our school and a little about the mining operation in the town of Bisbee. We had fifteen minutes to do it in.

Well, I was through about the same time as the other kids were and as soon as she had time to look the papers over our teacher said, "We have one very good paper and who do you think wrote it? It is Walter's paper and if I had not stood there and watched him write it, I would have given him an "F", just like I did on that poem he wrote. There is something wrong with it, however. Walter, your spelling is bad and your hand writing is no better, But if you will take it home and rewrite it, I will send it to the school in Kansas."

Well, I took that letter home and rewrote it so many times that I had it memorized and I thought I had it perfect, but when I handed it to the teacher, she looked

at it for a minute and said, "Vera, will you come to the
front of the room?"

Then she handed MY letter to Vera and said, "Here,
take this and rewrite it and then I will send it off."

This made me so mad that I made up my mind that I was
not going to study any more at all. If I couldn't be the
smartest kid in school, I sure could be the dumbest and
besides it was a whole lot easier.

The Football Hero

It was in the fall of 1928 and I was a going to the
Greenway School in Warren. School was out for the day and
I was a waiting for the bus to take me home, and sometimes
we had a long wait.

While we were a waiting, we sometimes played
football. I say "we". Well, I really meant the other
boys. Most of the time I was just a spectator.

There was another school some five or six miles away,
by the name of Horace Mann School, and they were always
trying to beat Greenway School at football. There was no
teacher or even a coach of any kind there to help us, just
a bunch of kids a playing football.

There was not even a very good place to play, for
that matter. There were some pretty big rocks in the
playground, in fact. And this game was that tough tackle
football. I guess that is part of the reason that I was
not a playing most of the time. I didn't want to get
hurt.

Well, before every game, all of the bigger kids would
get together and make up the ground rules and everybody
went by them. If they didn't go by the rules there was a
big fight.

On this particular day, I was on the sidelines a
watching, when one of the bigger kids said, "Swan, I want

155

you to play in the backfield."

He spoke with such firmness that I was afraid to say no. So I got into the game.

All I had to wear at that time was a pair of bib overalls and a shirt, and, of course, shoes with no sox. I was put together without buttons most of the time. In other words, safety pins held up my overalls. I got teased about that a lot.

Here I was a standing a way back there with my hands in my pockets, about half watching the game and the other half watching a marble game that was a going on on the sidelines, when I heard some one holler, "Swan!"

I looked up in time to see the football a coming at me. I threw up my hands to protect my face and, much to my surprise, I caught that football.

There were a whole bunch of big kids a running down the field after me and I knew that if I didn't start a running that I would be smeared all over those big rocks. So I really put it in high gear and was out running all of them. But pretty soon they caught up with me and down I went. But it was too late for them. I had made the winning touchdown and everybody was a hollering.

But I was more interested in getting myself put back together again 'cause I was about to lose my britches. In fact, they were all but off of me right then. I looked all around for the two safety pins, but I couldn't find them.

By now the bus had arrived and I had to hold onto both suspenders with both hands and watch out that I held onto them real tight so that some bigger kid wouldn't sneak up behind me and pull them off of me in front of the girls.

I got to the bus OK and I felt safe as soon as I sat down.

Well, I gained a reputation of being a football player and somewhat of a hero for making the winning

Me

Henry, me 'n Oliver

touchdown and that felt good.

I guess it pays to be in the right place at the right time, if you can.

The Lost Shoe

This particular afternoon I was a sitting in the classroom just a waiting for school to let out so I could go home. The teacher was trying to teach me something about how the Chinese raised rice in China. The class was called "Geography". It didn't make any difference to me what they called it and I sure wasn't interested in rice in China. I was just plain not interested in the least.

I was a looking around to see if there was something that I could do that might be entertaining. I glanced down at the floor in front of me and saw a shoe that belonged to the girl that was sitting just in front of me.

Boy, did her feet stink! I guess that is why she took her shoes off all of the time.

I kept a close eye on the teacher and reached my foot as far as I could to see if I could get it and slide it within reaching distance. And I did.

I picked it up and slipped it inside my shirt and thought that it would be funny if she couldn't find her shoe. So I took it and hid it in the waste basket in the cloakroom in back of the class room.

I had just returned to my seat when the janitor, Mr. Howard, came in and got the basket and hauled it off to the incinerator and burned the papers. And the shoe, too, I guess.

The teacher called on Elsie (that was the girl's name) to come to the front of the room and read to us out of the Geography book.

Elsie started a looking around for her shoe. "Where is my shoe? Someone stole my shoe!" she said.

I thought to myself, "I did that pretty smooth.
Nobody saw me."

The teacher started getting mad and said, "Nobody is
going to leave this room 'til that shoe is found."

Everybody was searched. Every desk was searched.
And still no shoe was found. The teacher was determined
that we were all going to stay after school 'til it was
found.

By now, I knew it was best for Walter to not say
anything and let the mystery of the lost shoe go unsolved.

We all stayed after school for a half hour or so 'til
the teacher finally let us go.

That poor girl had to go home with only one shoe.
She kind of hopped and walked as she went towards home.
She was a crying, too, for fear of what her parents would
do.

I was a feeling real bad now, 'cause I didn't mean to
cause her so much trouble, but I was too scared to say
anything. It had gotten out of hand and all I had wanted
to do was to break the monotony a little.

The next day, Elsie had washed her feet and had a new
pair of shoes. She never took them off again at school
and I never let monotony get the better of me again.

Quail Hunting With The Principal

In 1929 I was in the sixth grade. That was a hard
time for me in more ways than one.

In the first place, I was taller than all the rest of
the kids and I was at that age where I thought I was
smarter than the teacher and I was always getting sent to
the principal's office 'til we got to be pretty good
buddies.

I kind of looked forward to being sent there. In
fact, sometimes I would aggravate the teacher just to get

sent there. One day I managed to aggravate the music
teacher enough that she sent me to the principal's office.
That was just what I wanted.

As soon as I got to his office I was greeted with a,
"Hello, Walt. You're just the person that I want to see.
Do you know where there is any good quail hunting?"

It was December and quail season had just opened.

"I sure do." Then I started to tell him how to get
there.

But he interrupted me with, "Go get you hat and
lunch while I crank up the Model T and I'll meet you out
in front."

When I went back to my classroom, all of the kids
thought that I was in real big trouble, so I didn't tell
them any different.

I went out to the principal's car and got in the
front seat with him and we started out for Bisbee
Junction.

All of a sudden I said, "Hold everything! Right
over there about a hundred yards, there is a bunch of
quail."

So he pulled the car off the road and I followed him
over to where I said that they were. We came to them a
little sooner than I expected to and flushed them before
he was ready and he only got two.

We hunted around for more, but the quail were gone.

I said, "Let's go back to the car. I think I can
find another bunch."

Well, we hunted 'til about time for school to be let
out and then went back. Boy! That was sure a lot of fun.
A lot better than studying music. I never could sing
anyway.

It wasn't long after that that the teachers got wise
to what was a going on. So instead of sending me to the
principal's office, they kept me in at recess and made me
study. Now, boy that really hurt! I sure would rather be

out playing during recess.

Arithmetic

One day the teacher kept me in at recess and made me
do arithmetic – – long division. Boy! That was real hard.
I worked all recess on those problems and still didn't get
anywhere with them.

So the teacher said, "Well, Walter, you can take
them home to do them. If you get them all correct you can
play when recess comes tomorrow. If not, you will have to
stay in again."

When I got home that night I made a deal with my
mother. I said, "Mamma, if you will do my arithmetic I
will do all of the dishes for you."

It was my turn to do them, anyway. I didn't have
anything to lose, so she agreed on it and had them all
done by the time that I was done with the dishes. Then I
copied them.

I felt good the next day because I knew I would be a
playing ball come recess time.

But it didn't work out that way. You see, everyone
of those arithmetic problems was wrong!

The teacher said, "Walter, you stay in at recess
time and I will show you where you made your mistakes."

She was real patient with me. We went over every
problem and that pointed out the fact to me that my mother
couldn't add any better than I could. I guess that I came
by it naturally. I never told my mother about it or she
would never have helped me again.

CHAPTER 15

THE BURROS

My **Own** Burro

Me 'n another kid by the name of Cody were sitting on the back steps of the Greenway School eating our lunch. You see, we most always ate together 'cause he liked the homemade bread that my mother made sandwiches with, even if they were only peanutbutter and sour cream, and sometimes, honey. He always had all of the good stuff like baloney and mustard on store bread sandwiches and we would trade lunches sometimes.

While we were eating our lunch we would watch the bigger boys ride the burros. There was a whole bunch of them most of the time, more on the first part of the week than the last.

You see, the burros really didn't belong to them, but really belonged to the Mexican wood cutters, but it was an unwritten law in those parts that possession was ownership as far as the burros were concerned. That is, if you were big enough to defend your belongings.

As we were eating, Cody said, "Walter, did you ever ride a burro much?"

"Naw, not much, but I'll bet it's a lot of fun if you could stay on and get them to go. Some of them are so stubborn that all they do is just stand there," I ans – wered.

"I got a burro, Walter. You can have 'er if you want 'er. She's been a getting into my mother's garden and she said if I kept 'er out I could have it, but I'm getting tired of looking after 'er and if you want 'er you can have 'er, if you come and get 'er." Cody said.

"Man! That sounds like a good deal. When can I come and get 'er?"

"Oh, any time tomorrow, if you want."

By then the bell had rung and we had to go inside and study again.

Well, that evening, when I got home from school I asked my dad if I could have the burro that Cody didn't want any more and he said yes. So I made arrangements to get off the bus at his house instead of mine. You see, he lived a mile or so south of us, that is, as the crow flies, but around by the road it was a lot longer.

To get that burro home before dark would be a job and I didn't like to be out by myself after dark 'cause I was afraid of the dark, but I didn't want anybody to know about it.

As the bus approached Cody's house, I caught the smell of chicken a frying that his mother was fixing for supper. Boy, did that make me hungry! I guess I was hungry most of the time, anyway.

As we walked in the door Cody's mother said, "Hi, Walter, do you want to stay and have supper with us? It will be ready in a few minutes."

"Boy, yeah! We don't have fried chicken much at our house and I sure do like fried chicken." I said in a hurry.

We ate our fill of that good fried chicken and after supper we went to see if we could find the burro. After

looking for some time we spotted her some hundred yards
away and as soon as she saw us she made a beeline for a
big patch of cockleburs.

Cody yelled, "Head 'er off or she'll be so full of
those things that it will take you a week to get them all
out and you will never be able to ride her home."

He hadn't told me that she had a half grown colt,
too. Well, we finally caught her, but I forgot to bring a
rope or a bridle or anything to use to get her home with.

Well, me 'n him picked out cockleburs for about an
hour and had to give up 'cause it was getting along
towards sundown and I was getting real anxious to get
headed in the direction of home.

Cody loaned me a rope and instead of riding her home,
I lead her and her colt followed along behind.

We were a going along just fine. A little slow, but
that was to be expected. As we went over the overpass
that went over the railroad tracks a big covey of quail
flew up and flew into the telegraph wire and six of them
fell to the ground. I wanted them real bad but I was
afraid to stop to pick them up, but the more I thought
about it, the more I could imagine how they'd taste after
they were fried.

So I tied up the burro to a mesquite bush beside the
road and made a fast run down and got the quail and put
them inside my shirt and was on my way again.

But the burro decided that was all the farther she
was a going to go in that direction.

So I said, "I know what I'll do. I'll head her in
the direction that she wants to go and then tie my bandana
handkerchief over her eyes and see if that will work."
And it did!

It was way after dark when I got home and my dad was
starting to worry about me and was just about ready to
come a looking for me.

Mamma said, "Walter, do you want to eat some supper?

It's all cold now, but we saved you some, anyway."

But I wasn't hungry and I told her about Cody's mom's fried chicken.

Then Henry got jealous 'cause he didn't get any good fried chicken and he started a grumbling about him a having to do my share of the chores, feeding the chickens and gathering the eggs.

You see, we were in the chicken business together. We had a couple hundred laying hens. So I got in and helped him wash the eggs and carton them and get them ready for the market. Then he started feeling better and soon had forgotten all about it.

Chicken Feed

Well, I kept that burro around there for some time, but I never did try to get all of the cockleburs out of her.

One evening at the supper table, my dad was telling about one of the neighbors to the west of us, who had chickens and how many eggs he was a getting and the way he was a doing it.

You see, he had a lot of horses, and there was broomtail or two in among them. From time to time he would butcher one of them and feed the meat to his chickens.

That night, when I went to bed, I got to thinking, "That dumb burro has too many cockleburs and about all she is good for is chicken feed."

And the more I thought about it the more it sounded like a good idea.

"Well, tomorrow is Saturday. When everybody goes to town I'll make chicken feed out of both of those burros." I thought.

That was not as easy as I had it planned 'cause my

dad wanted to take me to town with him to get me a pair of
shoes. So I had to go with them, but the next Saturday, I
was left at home and as soon as the Model T was out of
sight, I got the knife and went to work.

It was not any where as easy as I thought it would be
to butcher a couple of burros. I had watched them butcher
cattle over at the Warren Ranch and that looked real easy.
So, you see, I thought I could butcher, too.

But by the time everybody got home from town, I had
the meat all cut up in small enough pieces that I could
handle and had them a hanging up on the north side of the
house where it got pretty cold at night.

Nobody paid much attention to what I had done while
everyone else was in town. Everything was a going about
normal around there 'til one Saturday some of the neighbor
boys came to see me and wanted to ride the burros for a
while and I said that it was impossible.

"Why is that, Walter?" they asked.

"Well, you see, I butchered them and I'm a feeding
the meat to the chickens." I answered.

Then I took them over and showed them where the
burros were a hanging up on the north side of the house.
They were real unhappy at me, to say the least. They said
that I had murdered the burros that they all liked to ride
so well and that I didn't have any right to do that.

Now I felt bad because of what I had done. I think
if they had been big enough they would have beat me up
right there. But they left and went home.

I Was In Trouble

When I went to school the next Monday. Every kid at
school knew about it and I was hated by all of the boys.
I was a burro killer and that was what they all called me.
I was in *DEEP* trouble.

I spent most of the time trying to keep from getting beat up by some of the bigger kids at the school.

There was a gang of big boys from the Lowell School that were to be there after school to beat me up and I heard about it. So I didn't study very hard and misbehaved so that the teacher would keep me in after school. She'd let me out just in time to catch the bus.

I knew what time the bus was to come from Lowell to pick up all of us kids and take us to Bisbee Junction. So when the teacher let me out to go home, I went to the boys restroom and looked out the window to see if there was any of those boys from the Lowell School a waiting for me like they said they would. And there sure were. There were six of them, and they were big and mean looking. I wanted to stay as far away from them as I could.

They were busy a playing marbles with some other big boys that didn't ride the bus and I figured if I ran as fast as I could to where the bus was a loading up kids that I could get there before they would see me.

Well, it worked! They didn't see me 'til I was almost to the bus and they didn't get there in time to get me before I got on the bus.

Boy, was I ever scared! I felt real bad that everybody hated me so. Even the girls didn't like me, either. It bothered me so much that I couldn't even sleep. That was all that I could think about. I was so worried about getting beat up the next day that I didn't want to go to school any more. I was sure that my dad would understand if I explained it to him and maybe he would let me stay home from then on.

He could see that I was scared to death of those big boys, so he let me stay home from school that day and showed me much love and kindness all day long.

There were two things that I learned that day that I have never forgotten. First, you can never run away from trouble and, second, that trouble always casts a shadow

before it happens. If you are smart you can always see
it. When I did go back to school, I had to stay out of
the way and watch my step to keep from getting beat up for
a couple of weeks.

CHAPTER 16

LIFE ON THE SWAN RANCH

The Wild Cow

Sometime about the time of the big depression our homestead began to be known as the *SWAN RANCH* by the townspeople. But life went on just about the same regardless of what our homestead was called.

One day, the last thing that our dad said to us before he left for work was, "You two boys get that stray white face cow out of the pasture. There isn't enough grass for our own cows, much less the strays."

So me 'n Henry went to great lengths to figure just how we were going to get her out of the pasture. But some how or other Henry always managed to use my chin to lead with instead of his. So I, being a little on the dumb side, took it all in.

The first thing that I did was to roll up my sleeves. I don't know why, unless it was that it made me feel a little bigger, 'cause that's what Daddy always did when he got ready to tackle a big job. I doubled up my fists and bowed my neck a little and started for the cow, swinging my fists by my side.

169

Henry was a way in back of me urging me on with, "G'over there and run at 'er, Walter!" So I did.

When I got within forty or fifty feet from her, she started to paw the dirt and blow her nose at me. Then she shook her horns. I was scared stiff and felt like rolling down my sleeves and going back to the house.

Then I heard Henry's voice from a way back, saying, "Bluff 'er, Walter. You can do it!"

So I took a deep breath and started for her again.

The next thing I knew was that I could see the whites of her eyes, and the rest looked like they were made of glass.

She wasn't bluffing very easy and one of us would have to give up pretty quick or I was going to start a running, but fast!

Then I heard a faint voice say, "Stay with 'er, Walter!"

And I made one more try at her, but I had to grab her horns to keep them out of my stomach. And I was a backing and a hoping I wouldn't fall. I was wishing that I could turn loose and run. But just then she fell down and I felt like Don Juan, the great bull fighter. She was in a pile on the ground!

Henry came a running up to me then and I said, "Look! That cow is sick. Look at 'er pant.!"

He said, "No, you just out bluffed 'er. You sure are strong, Walter. You stay here and hold her head down while I go get the rope. We'll put it around 'er horns and tie the other end on the old Model T and we can pull 'er out."

So I stood there a holding her horns. Pretty soon she stopped breathing so hard and got up. She looked at me kind of funny and ran off like a scared jackrabbit. So I walked back to the house.

By now, Henry had the well rope and took the butcher knife and cut the bucket off. When he saw me he said, "I thought I told you to hold that cow. Where is she now?"

"Down in the pasture, I guess." I answered.

"Well, Daddy said for us to get 'er out of there so we'd better do what he said." Henry said.

So he got the old Model T and we drove around the pasture 'til we found her. We both sat in the Model T and watched her 'til she went to sleep under the shade of a mesquite tree.

"Now, Walter," Henry said, "I'll drive up close to 'er and then you get out and put the rope around 'her horns and tie it good. Then come back here and I'll show you how to handle a wild cow!"

It was not too hard to get that rope around her horns and the other end tied to the back end of the Model T. The cow was still a sleeping like a baby.

Henry said, "I'll get this Ford in high gear and when the slack comes out of the rope, you watch that cow move."

I thought that he would snap that cow's head off, but the rope broke in the middle and it woke her up. She was mad and she looked as if she was a pawing with all fours. She started for the Model T and she hit the radiator with her horns. Water was going everywhere. Then she made a pass for the side of the Model T but she fell in a heap on the ground.

I said, "Let me get out and get the ten feet piece of rope off of 'er."

"Better not. She might kill you. She's a loco cow! Wait 'til Daddy gets home."

That was his usual song and dance when he got in a pickle. "Wait 'til Daddy gets home." So we went back to the house.

By now I was really thirsty, after all that activity. I said, "Let's go to the well and get a drink of cold water."

The water bucket was sitting on the edge of the well

and I had been so engrossed in the wild cow that I tossed
it in, not thinking that there wasn't a rope on it. It
hit the bottom with a splash.

Henry looked at me and said, "You sure are a
bonehead. Come on! Let's go to the house and get a warm
drink."

At the house there was just enough water in the
bottom of the bucket to half fill the dipper. We split it
between us. Now that I knew that there was no more
water, I sure got thirsty.

We were supposed to do the dishes and cook supper,
but there was no water. In one way I was happy, if you
know what I mean, but what was to come later spoiled it
all.

I heard a car door slam in the front yard and looked
out to see Daddy standing there. It seemed to me that he
knew what we did before we did it.

The first words that came out of his mouth was,
"What kind of a bonehead stunt were you a pulling with
that well rope that broke it?"

Right now I thought that if I kept still my big
brother would put his foot in it and maybe I could save a
little of my own skin this way. But he didn't say any –
thing.

Then my dad directed his question to me bared down on
each word. "Well, where is the other part of the well
rope?"

"Oh, it is on the head of that wild cow that we tried
to get out of the pasture like you told us to do. Look!
You can see 'er down there now, eating grass."

I tried to tell him what an encounter we had had with
that cow, but all I could get out of my dad was a
preoccupied grunt. He was so mad about that rope that I
don't guess that he heard what I was saying. And he still
didn't even know about the water bucket in the bottom of
the well.

172

We all started for the cow and as soon as we got within a hundred yards of her she started to run like a deer a holding her head to one side to keep the rope out of her feet. When she got to the fence she jumped it like it wasn't there and the last we saw of her she was a going over the hill with that piece of rope a dragging from her horns.

We all stayed pretty thirsty around there 'til Daddy could get back to town to buy another bucket and rope for the well.

Our Chicken Business

We had acquired an old Carter's five – hundred – egg incubator that was heated by a kerosene lamp. That was what kept the eggs warm 'til they hatched. It was a crude looking contraption to me and I could never figure out what made it work or how it kept the right temperature.

Well, anyway, we got some eggs to hatch on shares 'til we had a lot of baby chicks. We didn't have any place to keep them so that we could keep them warm so we had to keep them in the house 'til they got feathers enough to keep them warm. And that was a mess!!

We had to clean up after them at least once a day or the smell got so bad that you couldn't live in the house with them. My mother was sure glad when they got big enough to make it on the outside of the house.

You see, there were a lot of other things that liked chickens, too, that lived around there. Hawks were the worst of them all, I guess. The coyotes got a few and the skunks got some, too.

As soon as the roosters got to weigh a pound or so we would kill them and fry them and it was not long 'til we had only pullets left. It was truly a poor man's chicken ranch. We had all sorts of things for them to stay in,

173

from old barrels to concrete forms nailed together, and, of course, they had the run of the whole place.

By the time that they started a laying there was about two hundred of them.

They were white leghorns and they started to lay fairly young and they laid all over the place. It was like an Easter egg hunt every day when we went to gather the eggs. It was fun. That is, for a while.

As soon as they started a laying good we got a little money in and then we built some better houses for them and some good nests, too.

One evening, after supper was over, my dad called me 'n Henry over to him and talked to us. He told us that he was giving us the chickens and we were to take care of them and the family was to have what eggs they wanted and what chickens they wanted to eat.

This was a big deal as far as I was concerned. We were going to get rich 'cause the price of eggs was good at that time and there was a lot of eggs being laid every day. But we had to save the money to pay the feed man when he came with a load of feed.

Henry was afraid that I might spend some of it so he carried the money all of the time and this made me mad and I was always complaining about it to my dad. But it never got me anywhere. So I figured I would try something else and see if it would. I sure wanted a chance to carry that money. So I started a pouting.

I did this for a while and finally Henry came to me and said, "Walter, what is the matter with you?"

"I don't like the chicken business." I said,
" 'cause you get to carry the money all of the time and I never get to carry it at all."

Then he said, "I'll tell you what, Walter. If you go clean out all of the chicken houses, I'll let you carry the money for a whole day."

That sounded pretty good to me so I said, "That's a

deal!" And I went out and cleaned out the chicken houses.

When I was done I went to Henry and said, "Where's the money, Henry?"

And he said, "I'll let you have part of it."

That wasn't the deal! And all this did was to start a fight and we really went at it, that is, 'til Daddy saw us and stopped us.

He said, "What started all of this?"

I told him that Henry wouldn't let me carry all of the money like he said that he would. By now we were getting too big to whip, so he gave us both a good bawling out and let it go. When it was all over, I got to keep the money for a whole week instead of only one day.

It was quite a chore to shut the chickens up at night and we always tried to get it done before it got dark. There was a favorite radio program that came on about that time of day. It was "Frank Watanabe and the Honorable Archie" on Station K N X, Los Angeles, California. So if we didn't get them shut up before then, we would have to do it afterwards and that was not any fun 'cause we had to watch out for snakes.

This particular night when we went to shut the chickens up there was a skunk there eating one of the chickens in the corner of the chicken house. I guess it was too big for the skunk to drag it out of there. That was the only chicken in there. All the rest of them were scattered out in the brush and we were afraid to go out there in the dark 'cause it was summer and there was a lot of rattlesnakes out there. We would rather let the bobcats and coyotes have a few of them than to take a chance of getting bitten by a snake. From then on we shut them up as soon as they went to roost.

We had one hen that had some little baby chicks. She was a roosting in an old barrel not too far from the house. Henry was supposed to shut them up, but instead he was listening to the radio.

In the middle of the program, he looked at me and said, "Walter, will you go shut up the hen for me?"

I was about half asleep and I said, "Sure." And I went out of the house without any shoes on, on a dead run 'cause I was always afraid of the dark. Anyway, when I got about halfway there, right under my feet a rattlesnake started a rattling and a telling me that I was too close to him.

I turned and stepped as high as I could and flew back into the house. If fright could have killed me, I would have been dead that night.

As soon as I was in the house everybody in there knew what had happened. Daddy got the twelve gauge shot gun and went out and shined the car lights on the snake and shot it. It was one of the biggest snakes that I ever saw, I do believe, and I was sure glad I managed to get out of his way.

I was always glad to see cold weather come. There were no snakes then.

As soon as it got cold, the chickens slowed down their egg production and we were not getting so many eggs. Henry was a big – brothering me so much that I said that I wanted out of the chicken business.

I said, "Do you want to buy me out?"

Well, he didn't have any money, either.

I think that he wanted me out, though, 'cause he said, "I'll tell you what I'll do. We'll divide up the hens. I will take all of the ones that are a laying and you can have all of them that are not a laying. You put yours down at the garden and I'll keep mine at the house."

I was sure that I was a getting the short end of the deal, but I wanted out and so I agreed to it.

When it was all done and settled, I had twice as many hens as Henry did, but he was the one that was a getting all of the eggs and all I was a doing was feeding mine and getting nothing out of them. So I figured the only way

that I could get any eggs was to take real good care of
them and feed them real good.

I even went and got a couple of burros, butchered
them, and fed the chickens the burro meat. This did the
trick. It was not long 'til they were a laying real good.

By now, all of Henry's hens had almost stopped
laying. Now I had the money. I was a selling eggs all
over the town of Warren and my front pocket was bulging
with money.

But, somehow, by the time that I had paid for the
chicken feed, there wasn't much money left. So I wound up
a selling all of my hens to the P.D. store in Warren and I
divided the money up with Henry.

Traps In The Well

One morning, my dad sent me to find the young
Holstein bull that had not come up for several days. I
hunted half a day before I found him and he was dead. He
was to the west and south about a half mile from the
house.

Daddy went to where he was and looked at him. He
decided that the burro that belonged to the neighbors just
south of us must have run him to death. He was a good
bull and we needed him for all of the cows that we had at
this time, but he was gone now.

Well, I went all on my own to set some traps around
this dead bull. I set fifteen all around him. I did it
in a hurry and didn't do a very good job of it. I figured
that if there was enough of them that the coyotes would be
sure to step in one of them. I didn't tell my dad anything
about it at all.

The next morning, bright and early, I went down to
see if I had caught anything. Getting within a few
hundred feet, I could see a lot of dark objects in the

traps and I ran to the house to tell my dad that I had set traps around this dead bull and that there was a skunk in every trap and to get the twenty – two rifle and help me go get them.

He said, "This is the wrong time of the year to set traps. The hides are no good in the summertime, but let's go and get them out of the traps, anyway."

We started down to where the traps were set and as we got closer to them, we could see that everyone of them had a crow in it. So we got them all out and took all of the traps back to the house and put them up.

But the next day I got them down again and set a few of them by an ocotillo fence to see what I could catch, just for the fun of it.

I caught something, alright, and this time it was not a crow. It was a big cat! I knew it was a wild cat, so I went to the house and said to my dad that I had a wild cat in a trap and to come quick.

He said, "How do you know that it is a wild cat?"

"Oh, it is as wild as all get out and it's making a wild noise." I answered.

Daddy was the one that was wild instead of the cat. I had caught the neighbors cat by the hind foot.

We had a devil of a time a getting that cat out of that trap without getting all scratched up. As soon as the job was done, the cat went limping off toward the neighbors house.

This time the traps were put up again and I was given strict orders not to get them down again 'til it was winter time, then I could go trapping.

Well, it seemed as though winter would never get there and I forgot all about those traps after a while.

One morning Daddy said, "Do you want to set those traps now?"

I said, "Sure, you bet I do!"

So he shot some jackrabbits for me and I really

worked hard to do a good job setting the traps. This was
the first time that I was really left on my own. The year
before, I was allowed to set only one. I spent the
biggest part of the day getting them all set and I knew
for sure that I would have every one of them full in the
morning.

Well, when morning came, I went to see if I had
caught anything. And do you know what I saw? There was a
stick in every one of those traps.

This made me mad and I knew who did it. Or, at
least, I thought I did. So I went to where this other guy
was a trapping and as fast as I came to his traps, I would
snap them and would take them up 'til I had all of them.
They were heavy, too, and hard to carry. I took them over
to an old hand – dug well that had been abandoned and threw
them in it. Then I went back and gathered up all of mine
and went home.

I never told a soul that I did this, but I kept
thinking a way back in my mind what my dad had said to me
one time when we were walking all alone on a hunting
jackrabbits trip.

"Walter, what ever you do will always come back to
you whether it is good or bad, and most of the time it
will come back ten times over."

Well, I went through many years and nobody stole any
of my traps, but I want you to know that one morning, when
I went to check a string of my traps that was about twenty
miles long, all of my traps were gone except one. The
only reason that it wasn't taken, too, I guess, was 'cause
it was one too many to make ten times that number that I
threw in that well some forty years before.

Gathering Coal

It was a Saturday morning and we had just finished

breakfast. Me 'n Henry had great plans for a big fun day.

But that was quickly changed by my mother when she said, "I want you two boys to get some wood for the cook stove. I've got to bake bread today."

So we hurried to bring in some wood so we could go play.

Mamma looked at the wood we had brought in and then looked outside where the wood pile was and said, "Is that all the wood that you brought me?"

We didn't answer, hoping that we could get away with it.

But she said, "Boys, what did you do? Go rob a crow's nest? That isn't even wood! Now go and get me some real wood!"

"Can we go along the railroad tracks and pick up the coal that has fallen off of the engines?" we asked.

"Well," she said, "Yeah, I guess so."

So we both got a gunny sack and started for the railroad track that was about a mile away.

When we finally got to the tracks Henry said, "I think that was a dumb idea of yours. I'm already tireder than if I had chopped wood. Well, we're here now so we might as well see if we can find some coal."

There really wasn't much coal along the tracks. I think that some of the neighbor kids were there ahead of us. We gathered coal for about an hour and we looked up ahead and saw one of the neighbor boys a picking up coal, too.

We soon caught up to him, and saw that he didn't have as much coal as we did.

He said, "This is a slow way to get coal. Why don't we go up to the coal bin at the station and fill our sacks?"

Me 'n Henry didn't like the sounds of this too well 'cause we were taught better, but we were a getting pretty thirsty and one of us said, "We'll go to the railroad station with you to get a drink. You can do what you want to."

So we carried our coal with us 'til we got within a few hundred feet of the station. Then we hid it in some grass. Then we went up to the station to get a drink.

While we were getting a drink, the neighbor kid went to the coal bin and was a filling up his sack, when the railroad bull (that was what we called the railroad security officer) caught him and made him dump it all out. He told him that if he ever caught him there again he would kick his seaterumpus.

After we saw what happened to the neighbor boy, we started to leave for home.

That railroad bull called to us and said, "Boys, have you got some coal, too?"

We said, "Yes, but we picked it up along the tracks."

He said, "Yeah, Unh, unh. Well, go get it and dump it in the bin and don't either of you come back again."

We tried to tell him we didn't steal it, but he didn't listen to us. So we took our empty sacks and got another drink and headed for home.

That mile and a half was sure a long one by now.

By the time we had gotten home, our mother was trying to bake bread with those little sticks we had left her.

We sat down and told her what had happened and all she said was, "Boys, it's not enough to be honest, you have to avoid the appearance of dishonesty."

A Boyish Prank

In the spring it was a yearly thing that we would extract the honey from the bees. That was after the mesquite bloom was over. It was real nice honey. I guess there is none better. We didn't have a very good place to extract the honey, but we got it done some how. A lot of the times a friend who had bees, too, would come over and help us. Then we would help him with his bees.

Well, this particular time we went out in the morning and took off all of the honey and had brought it all in. It was time for lunch and my mother usually fixed a good one.

After lunch, Stoner (that was the name of the man who was helping us) said, "I think I'll take a little nap before we start extracting that honey."

And my mother said, "Why don't you go to the boys room and lay down? There's not too many flies there if you keep the door closed."

Now this room was a tin shack about fifty yards from the house and not much bigger than eight by ten feet. It had a dirt floor, no windows and one door that was real hard to open and shut.

Well, Stoner went in there and me 'n Henry helped him close the door and it wasn't long 'til he was a snoring. I don't know how he could sleep when it was so dadgum hot in there, but I guess he had his choice. It was either the flies or the heat.

Me 'n Henry were a playing marbles close by and we heard him a snoring and this really tickled us.

I looked over and saw that the bee smoker was still a smoking a little and I said to Henry, "Hey! I know how we can have some fun. Let's smoke old Stoner out of there."

"OK", he said, and he went and got some more gunny sack and we really fired up that bee smoker. Then we opened a little crack in the door and I really poured in the smoke 'til my hands were tired. Then I gave it to Henry and he would puff it 'til he was tired.

By now, Stoner had stopped snoring and we could hear him a stirring a little.

I said to Henry, "We'd better clear out of here!"

So we dropped the smoker about where we had found it

and ran over and hid down in the grass to watch the show.

Pretty soon we could hear Stoner a hollering, "FIRE! FIRE!" And he finally beat his way out. When he got outside he was still a hollering, "FIRE!"

My dad heard him and he came a running with a bucket of water. They both went in there to put out the fire.

By now, me 'n Henry were a laughing so hard and so loud that my dad heard us. He called us over to him and did he ever give us a whipping and a good bawling out!

But I still think it was worth it.

Our Fireplace

Me 'n Henry were a sleeping in a little corrugated tin building some fifty yards from the house. It was pretty small, but it was big enough for a bed, and me 'n Henry both slept in the same bed. It was real cold in the wintertime and down right hot in the summertime.

One night we were a talking before we went to sleep. We decided to dig a cellar to sleep in. Maybe that would be the answer to all of our cold and hot problems. We had a two week Christmas vacation a coming up and we decided we would spend all of that time a digging a cellar.

We got some help from our dad 'cause he thought it was a good idea, too. But we were a long ways from getting it finished in those two weeks. It was some time in February before we finally got it finished.

It was about six feet deep and ten feet across by eighteen feet long. We got some railroad ties and covered over the top. Then we shoveled the dirt back on the top. We made some stairs to get down into it. It had a dirt floor, of course, and all of the walls were dirt, too. but it was real cozy down there.

I said to Henry, one night, "All we need is a fireplace in the wall, then we could build a fire in here and that sure would be nice."

So the next day, we spent a making a fireplace in the west wall. We dug out a place on the wall about two feet square and took the post hole digger and drilled a hole down for a chimney. It sure did look sharp and we were real proud of ourselves.

I wanted to build a fire in it right away, but Henry said, "Let's wait 'til it gets dark and spend all the rest of our time a getting some wood."

So I did what he wanted and helped him go get some wood. We got quite a bunch of it.

That night, we went down in our cellar to go bed as soon as the sun went down. I know that it was not even good and dark, yet, when we built a fire in our new fireplace.

I got some paper and filled it to the top with wood and lit it. It started to burn pretty good, then it started to smoke. We tried to fan the smoke up the chimney, but that didn't do any good. So we went to bed and covered our heads.

I said, "It will soon go away and be real nice in here."

Then Henry said, "You just don't know how to build a fire!"

Well, we stayed there as long as we could. We both started a coughing and the tears were a running from our eyes.

I said to Henry, "We're going to have to get out of here. The smoke is too bad."

He said, "I can stand it longer than you can, I'll bet."

Well, I didn't want to bet with him and I got out of there. I didn't even take time to pick up my britches. But as soon as I got outside, I was wishing I had of 'cause my behind was a getting cold.

It wasn't two minutes 'til here came Henry, but he

took time to get his britches.

I wanted to go back in there and get mine, but the smoke was so bad I just stayed there and shivered.

I said, "I know what! Let's set fire to the wood pile that we got here and keep warm 'til the smoke goes out of there." So we did.

Daddy heard the commotion and came out of the house to see what was going on and there I stood without any britches on and we were a laughing and having a lot of fun.

All he said was, "What in the world are you burning up all of that wood for, anyway? That's enough to make a batch of bread."

Our covers smelled of that smoke for a long, long time. It wasn't 'til years later when I learned more about fireplace construction that I found out why that fireplace smoked so bad.

CHAPTER 17

PIGS, POLLYWOGS, & GARDENS

My Pig Business

    May was a beautiful time of the year. It wasn't cold
any more and it hadn't gotten hot, yet. The mesquites were
a blooming, and this added to the good feeling one had
when he got up in the morning. To top it all off, school
would be out in a few weeks and I could go barefooted
again. My feet had outgrown my shoes and they were about
worn out, anyway. I figured if I could get me a job and
work all summer long that I might be able to send off to
Sears & Roebuck to get me a real good pair of shoes for
next winter.

    The very afternoon that school was out, I started a
looking for a job. We lived a mile from the closest
neighbor and it was four miles to town. So I chose to go
to the neighbors to look for a job.

    About all I knew how to do was to pull weeds or cut
wood and clean up yards and all of those jobs didn't pay
very much 'cause there were neighbors who lived south of
the border that would work for just something to eat.

    Well, I started out knocking on doors and asking for

a job. I was scared to death to do this. It felt a
little like jumping into a pond of cold water. Most
usually there was a dog in the yard trying to tell me that
I was not wanted there.

I walked into one yard and there was a great big
black dog that jumped at me and I froze there. I could
not move an inch. Pretty soon the lady of the house came
out and called off the dog and as soon as I could talk I
told her that I wanted work.

I said, "I want to work for you a pulling weeds or
cleaning up your yard so I can get a little money to get
me a pair of shoes."

I think that she felt bad that her dog had scared me
so bad and she gave me the job. My wages were to be fifty
cents a week. This was good. If I worked all summer I
could have enough money to get the shoes I wanted.

I think that I ran most of that mile home to tell my
dad the good news.

The next morning I was up at daylight and I walked
all the way down to my new job and was there before anyone
was even out of bed. I went out in the garden and was a
pulling weeds when the lady saw me working out there.

She went to the back door and said, "Walter, do you
want to come in and have breakfast with us?"

This sounded real good to me 'cause I had left home
without eating a thing. All we would be having was some
cornmeal mush and I was so tired of eating that, I would
just as soon go without as to eat it.

But when I got home that evening, after a days work,
I wished that I had eaten 'cause my dad said, "Walter,
did you leave here without eating anything at all?" And I
told him that I had, but the neighbor fed me.

Then he said, "That is the last time that I want you
to do that. I don't want the neighbors to think that you
are not fed here at home."

I would just as soon have eaten at the neighbors all

summer 'cause she sure could make good pancakes.

After about two weeks, my mother said to me, "Walter, you'll have to stay home today from work. I just have to wash those britches. They are filthy."

It was going on three weeks since they were washed. You see, that was the only pair I had.

I hated washday because I had to gather wood or dry cow chips, or anything that would burn, then I'd made a fire under the black tub in the back yard to heat the water. Then I'd have to take off my britches and go to bed 'til they were washed and got dry again.

I hated to stay in bed, but I hated for my sisters to see me worse. That was a long day, but it was all over with 'til they got dirty again.

I sure was glad to get back to work. Well, I worked all that summer and I figured that I had about twelve dollars a coming to me. Look at all of the britches and shoes that would buy!

When I finished my work, the time had come to go collect my money, but when I asked the lady for it she said, "Walter, I don't have any money at all. The best I can do is to give you a couple of little pigs."

I was disappointed, but pigs would be better than nothing. So she helped me put them in a gunny sack, but they were too heavy for me to carry.

I said, "Let me carry one home, and I'll be back after the other one."

It took me a good hour to get home carrying that pig over my back.

When I got home with it my dad said, "Did you get paid?"

I smiled and said, "Yes, I got two pigs. I got to go back and get the other one. One is a little sow and the other is a little boar."

Daddy didn't have the heart to tell me what he really thought, but he went with me to get the other one. He even helped me make a pen for them.

After that was done, he said, "What are they going
to eat, Walter"

" 'Skeet beans, I guess." I answered. I sure didn't
have any money to buy feed for them. So for a week I
gathered mesquite beans to feed them.

School had started by then and it was hard to find
time to gather all the mesquite beans those two pigs could
eat. Then I got a bright idea!

"Why don't I save the lunch scraps from all the kids
at school? That will feed them!" I thought.

Well, this was agreeable with my dad, the teacher,
and the principal, so I got me a ten pound lard bucket and
saved all of the lunch scraps. This was enough to feed
only one pig, so my dad killed the boar pig and we ate it.

Sometimes, coming home from the bus stop, I would get
pretty hungry. You see, it was a mile from the house to
where the bus stopped to pick us up in the morning and let
us off in the afternoon. So I would take the lid off the
lard bucket and see what there was good to eat in there.
This was a pretty good snack to hold me 'til supper time.

I kept eating less and less supper all of the time,
'til one evening, my mother said, "Walter, I'm worried
about you. You aren't eating very good lately. Aren't
you feeling good?"

I said, "I'm fine."

But she said, "Stick out your tongue." So I did.

Then she said, "Umm. Just as I thought. You're
bilious! Well, you'll feel a lot better after I give you
a good physic."

So down went two tablespoons of caster oil. Then I
sure didn't feel good. After that I ate my supper even if
I wasn't hungry.

Well, I managed to feed that little pig all winter
long and she grew up to be a good sized sow. I figured
that I would like to go into the pig raising business so I

took her to a neighbors to have her bred. When she had
her little pigs there were eight of them.

This made me feel like I was a big pig farmer.
Everybody that would listen to me, I would tell them about
my little pigs and this paid off.

One day a man drove into the yard in a truck and
asked if I had some little pigs to sell. I wasted no time
a showing them to him and he bought them all. He gave me
five dollars for each of them and I felt real rich.

I did save one of them for myself, though. That one
was a little sow. She was different from all the others.
She didn't know how to grunt. Instead of saying "Oink"
she said "Ink" so I called her Inky.

Inky got to be a real friend of mine. She was my
pet. Everywhere I would go she would follow me. I didn't
have a dog, so she was a good substitute. Whenever I
would go hunting for rabbits for breakfast, she would
follow me. If I was to stop and rest, she would find a
soft place and root her out a little place to take a nap
'til I was ready to go again.

There were times when she wanted to come into the
house, but my mother drew the line there. I do believe
that Inky could understand me when I would talk to her.
She would answer me right back with an "Ink".

When wintertime came and it got pretty cold at night,
every time my dad looked at my big sow, Inky's mother, you
could see pork chops a shining in his eyes and you could
see that he was not thinking about raising any more little
pigs. I had the feeling that as soon as the weather got a
little colder, she would turn into bacon and pork chops.

And that is just what happened. One day, when I came
home from school, there she was a hanging upside down from
a big mesquite tree. All she was now was pork. This made
me feel real sad, but I still had Inky, and as soon as she
grew up, I could start into the pig business all over
again.

I wouldn't eat a bite of that pork and I moped around the house for a long time. I wouldn't even talk to my dad.

One day he said, "Walter, as soon as I get enough money I'll buy you a boar and some sows and you can go into the pig business again." And he explained to me how he had to think about feeding his family and this was the only way he could do it at this time.

Now this made me feel better to hear this and I was on speaking terms with him again.

One day I was getting ready to go hunting and I called Inky, but she didn't come a running to me like she usually did. I looked all over for her and when I finally found her she was a laying behind the shed. I spoke to her and she just let out a very little "ink".

I went over to her and felt her. She was as hot as could be and looked real sick. I went and got my dad.

He looked at her and said, "I think that she has pneumonia. She looks pretty sick. Give her all of the water she will drink."

But she would not drink or eat anything. I covered her up with a blanket and did everything that I knew of for her, but the next morning, she was dead.

That was a sad day in my life. I felt like I had lost all of my best friends and there was no hope of ever getting back into the pig business again.

I put Inky into the wheelbarrow and hauled her off. I buried her real deep so that the coyotes couldn't eat her. There never again was a little pig that could take the place of Inky.

My dad did buy me some more pigs some years later. He did hold true to his promise that he made to me.

"me 'n Henry"

Me 'n Oliver, my little brother, with one of
little pigs I worked for.

Pollywogs

It was awful dry and I wish that there was some other word that I could use to describe it better. We would watch a billowy cloud a way off in the horizon, getting a little bigger and bigger, hoping that it would come over our way and cut loose and rain a little. But no, it always seemed to go off to Mexico and rain cats and dogs down there. We could see the flickering of the lightning and once in a while we could hear a faint sound of the thunder. Oh, what a wonderful place that Mexico must be!

We had a spot picked out for a garden and dug a bunch of little ditches diverting them into one big one, hoping to catch all of the water that fell, when it did come.

One morning, when I got up, I saw some big thunderheads in the south. I was a happy boy. I ran back into the house and reported the news to the rest of the family who were all still asleep.

My feelings were somewhat hurt when Daddy said, "Ah, shut up and go on outside."

So I did, and I sat in the wheelbarrow and sniffed that good air. I knew as sure as I was a sitting there that we were going to get a gully washer.

I felt a big drop of moisture on my cheek and I had a funny feeling. Maybe you have felt that way at some time or other. I hoped it would rain and, yet, was afraid that it wouldn't

You see, if it did, that meant that there would be water in the puddle hole and we could go swimming, sort of a mud bath swim, but a swim, anyway.

As soon as the big drops started to hit the tin roof on the house, the whole family got excited and started to holler.

That was the best rain that we'd had so far that year. It wasn't a gully washer, but everybody was so pepped up about it that we worked all morning a planting in the garden, in hopes that it might come back in the afternoon and really rain.

Well, about two that afternoon it started to sprinkle a little. All of the rest of the family had gone to town except me 'n Mamma. It started to come a little harder, and then harder, as I was watching out the window.

Soon the water started to run in the front yard a little, so I pulled off all my clothes and put on a ragged pair of overalls.

I said to Mamma, "Let's go and run the water onto the garden."

So she put on a pair of Daddy's pants and we started for the garden.

By now, it was really coming down and the lightning was a cracking everywhere. I was as busy as anything with that shovel, slopping in the mud with mud from head to toes, but the garden was getting wet and that was the main thing.

I caught a quick glance at Mamma and she looked worried. I knew she didn't like the lightning very much and the rain was a coming down in sheets now.

Pretty soon I heard her say, "The garden has enough water. Break the ditches and let the water go."

Just then a blinding flash hit a soapweed between us. I fell in the mud and as soon as I could get to my feet I was up.

I heard Mamma half scream and half holler, "WALTER!"

I was sure that she was hurt and she thought I was killed. We both were scared stiff and we hightailed it for the house as fast as we could go.

We got into some clean dry clothes and sat by the window to watch it rain.

Do you know that our garden was a river by then? It took all of the top soil and all of the seeds that we had planted that morning down into Mexico.

But it was not all gloom. There was the puddle hole

and it was full of water. I didn't mind so much not
having something to eat as long as I could have a good
time a swimming.

At daylight the next day, I was ready to go puddling
in the puddle hole, but Mamma had a different idea. So we
compromised and I waited 'til it was good and warm and all
five of us kids went in.

The water was fairly clear. That is, 'til we got in
it. There were a bunch of toads in there, too, just a
croaking to the top of their voices. They were sure happy
that there was a rain. They soon disappeared when the
water started to splash and kids started to yelling.

But our fun didn't last long, 'cause the water was
soon more mud than water. Then we all got out and started
for the house. We stopped by the well and drew some water
with a bucket and threw it on each other to wash a little
of the mud off.

I had to work the next few days and didn't get a
chance to go to the puddle hole and I was very much afraid
that the place had dried up, for it was awful hot and that
thirsty sun had sucked up most of the moisture on the
surface.

I put a very convincing argument that the work I was
a doing could wait 'til I took a little dip and Mamma took
the course of least resistance and said yes.

Oh Boy! I was happy and wasted no time in getting
there. I pulled off my clothes. No swim suit was
necessary. No one was around. (That is the reason I
liked to go by myself.)

Then I said to myself, "Hey, I'd better go look and
see if there is any water in there before I get too
excited."

Do you know, I looked over the bank and what do you
think I saw? Yes, there was water, but it was as green as
grass with a green scum over the top.

Well, there was but one thing to do and that was to

put those clothes back on and go back to the house.

I was pretty unhappy, but I went back and took one more look at the water before I started for the house.

"Well, what do you know?" I said, "There's some pollywogs! I'll go get me a jar and take some of them back to the house with me."

Well, I fooled around there for thirty minutes or so and got me a couple dozen of them and started for the house a whistling at the top of my voice.

When I walked in the door, Mamma said, "Did you have a nice swim, Walter? I see you're happy."

"Nope, but I got me a jar full of pollywogs. The water was too green for me. Hey, Mamma! Can I use your tea strainer? I want to put some clean water on them."

"Not on your life!"

"Then how about letting me use that lard bucket? We don't need two of them for water."

She agreed to let me use one of them if I would get all of my work done first.

I got in the water from the well, fed the chickens, and gathered the eggs. Then I went about the job of putting the pollywogs in the clean water in that lard bucket.

Pretty soon I heard my dad say to take the bucket down to the well and get some more water. The girls had used all of it on the dishes. I heard him all right, but you know, those were very interesting pollywogs and I forgot all about the water he told me to get and went to bed.

In the wee hours of the morning, I was awakened by somebody a coughing and a gagging in the other room. I had the funniest feeling in the pit of my stomach. I knew what had happened.

Mamma jumped up out of bed and said, "What's the matter, Bert?"

"Ah, I just swallowed some more of Walter's blue

belly pollywogs!" he said, "That's the second time and
the last time I've had a taste of his pollywogs."

And he grabbed the bucket and tossed the rest of the
water and pollywogs out the window.

From then on I was forced to keep all my pollywogs in
a can outside.

The Garden

As I was a walking home from school, I noticed my dad
a walking around in the mesquite brush just south of the
house some quarter of a mile. At first I didn't give much
thought to it 'til I noticed that he had a green mesquite
stick in his hand. It was a funny looking thing, about an
inch in diameter and about a foot long and it was forked.

He was a talking to himself like he did many times
before, but this seemed a little different. This time he
was a passing back and forth and he would go to the left a
little, then to the right a little, then he would say,
"It has to be right there!" Finally, he stopped.

I asked him what he was a doing and he said that he
was witching a well.

"Witching a well! What does that mean?" I asked.

"Well, you see, Walter, you take this stick and you
hold it in your hands like this and you walk around and
where the water is the closest to the surface, it will
point down. Look! I'll show you." And it pointed to
the same spot every time.

"What do you want to dig another well for? We have
one already." I asked him.

Well, do you see all of this nice loamy soil around
here? I think that would raise a good garden." He
answered.

It sure looked like an impossible job to ever do
anything when all you had to work with was a pick and a

shovel and I told him so.

Then he said that when you get hungry you can do a lot of things that you never thought you could do before and we were a getting to that point. If we didn't start raising some of the stuff that we ate we would be a going hungry soon.

You see, the great depression was a bearing down pretty heavy on us by then and our diet was getting rather limited and it was past time for us to do something about it.

Well, the next day when I got home from school and after I got me a bite of bread and honey, I went down to see what Henry and Daddy were a doing. They had dug a hole some four or five feet deep and about four feet across. It seemed pretty easy digging. So I got in there and had my turn at the pick. We worked there 'til dark then went to the house.

I tried to talk Daddy into letting me stay home from school to help them dig on the well, but it fell on deaf ears.

"You have all day Saturday to dig on the well." He said.

"But it's no fun a working on Saturday." I said. But what I said didn't do me any good.

By the time that Saturday came the well was a lot deeper. The deeper we got, the more moist the dirt was, even though it wasn't very deep yet, not anywheres near deep enough for a well. It was only about eight or nine feet deep and most of the water around there stood at about thirty – five or forty feet.

Well, do you know what? We struck water that Saturday at ten and a half feet and this made everybody excited. We worked as long as we could by bailing out the water. Then we had to think of something else or a better way of getting out the water so we could deepen the well.

There was a fellow down in the valley near Hereford

who had owed my dad some money for pasture rent for some years and it looked as if Daddy would never get his money. He had a well that had a pump in it. The windmill had long since been blown over and was gone, but there was some fifteen feet of two inch pipe and a pump at the bottom of it.

While I was at school Daddy and Henry went down there and got the pipe and pump from him in exchange for the money he owed Daddy. They had it there by the time I got home from school.

We changed the leathers in it by making some out of an old shoe. That worked pretty good. Now we could go deeper with the well.

You see, we pumped by hand' til all of the water was out, then we would go down and dig like crazy 'til we had to pump it out again, and repeat the process 'til we got the well deep enough to suit us.

The next big job was to get some of the brush off so that we could plant a garden. I guess we cleared off an acre or so. We got all of the mesquite tree stumps out and did out best to level it up.

We didn't have a whole lot of water. I guess it was somewhere around five gallons a minute. That is, if you pumped real hard and fast. So that would not take care of much garden.

The weather was getting warmer by now and school was out. Daddy had scraped together all of the money he could find and sent to a seed company back east and got a bunch of different kinds of seeds.

We planted a lot one day and I asked my dad why we had planted so much.

"Well," he said, "we have to allow for the rabbits eating their share and then there will be some left for us."

You see, we didn't have a fence around it.

Well, this sounded like a good idea, but it didn't

work out this way. The rabbits were a getting more than
their share and there would soon be none left for us.

So we started shooting the rabbits and eating them.
This was alright, but it seemed like the more we shot, the
more they came. Then they started a coming in at night.
So we started staying out there at night and shooting them
with the aid of a Model T headlight rigged up to a
battery. Even this was a losing battle.

One day I said to Daddy, "Did you notice where I put
the guts to the last rabbit I dressed that they haven't
eaten anything for some ten feet around them?"

You see, I was using the guts for fertilizer and that
was how we got the idea to sprinkle all of the vegetables
with a solution of rabbit guts. Sometimes we would let
them stand for a day or two to get good and ripe and then
use it. That worked real good, but we had to do it every
night. Boy, that was quite a job to do every evening.

One day I said, "Let's build a fence."

"Out of what?" was the reply that I got from Daddy
and Henry.

"Well, we went this far with nothing. We can build a
fence the same way."

And this is the way we did it.

We got some old mining cable and unraveled it. There
were four strands in it. When we took it apart, that gave
us enough wire to go around the garden with one on the
top, one on the bottom, and one in the middle.

Then we took the little old Model T truck and went
over on the hills by Gold Gulch and cut ocotillos. There
were a lot of them on the hills around there. They look a
little like a broom stick with a lot of sharp thorns on
them.

Well, we would stand these ocotillo sticks upright
and wire them to the three strands of cable we had, using
bailing wire from the nearby dairy to do this.

Our garden and ocotillo fence.

The SWAN RANCH where me 'n Henry grew up.

This made a pretty good fence and kept the rabbits out pretty good. Sometimes they would find a place to get through and then I would set a trap there and we would have meat to eat with our vegetables.

Then the quail would fly over the top of the fence and they would help themselves to our garden. They were troublesome 'til, one day, I figured out a way to catch them.

Well, you see, we had a big junk pile over the hill and that is where we went to get stuff to make things out of. Well, that is what most people would have called it, but we had another name for it.

I looked all over for something to make a quail trap. After a while, I found just the thing. It was a contraption that Daddy had made some years before to keep the little kids away from the hot cook stove so that they wouldn't get burned. It was a kind of a fence. Now, all I had to do was to stretch wire over it and I would have it made and that was real easy.

Just about the time that I had it made, Henry walked up and said, "What in the world do you think you're a making there, Walter?"

And I said, "A quail trap!"

"A quail trap? What are you going to catch? Fool's quail? A quail would be a fool to get into anything like that!"

"I bet it will work." I said, not letting his criticism bother me.

So I set my quail trap in the middle of the cabbage patch. That is where they came and bothered the garden the most. Then I fixed myself up a blind so that I could watch them. I figured that as soon as they all got in, I would rush the trap and then I would have them.

You know, I sat there for the longest time a waiting for them to come in and was about ready to give up and go to the house to get me something to eat, when here they

came, a whole bunch of them! And they were headed right
for my trap! I was so excited I could hear my heart a
pounding. I was sitting as still as I could so that they
wouldn't see me.

Pretty soon, one went into the trap, then another,
and they started a going in there real fast. By now there
was just five left to go in. Then one more went in, and
three went out, then five went out and four more went in.
And do you know, I sat there and let them all go out of
that trap.

Then here came a blue darter hawk and they all flew
for the brush. I sure wasn't about to let Henry know
about this 'cause he would have said that I was the fool
and not the quail.

Well, I made a few minor adjustments to my trap and
went to the house and got me a honey sandwich and fed the
pigs.

Then I went back there to see if my adjustments would
do the trick. As soon as I got within a hundred yards of
the trap, the quail saw me and started a flying, but this
time they were in the trap. They were trying so hard to
fly out of there that I thought they would all fly off
with that it.

I sure was tickled. I took them all out and killed
and dressed them and got them ready for supper. In fact,
I had them all fried and ready to eat when Daddy and Henry
came home from work.

I had them covered over with a dish towel and I had
cooked some other stuff, too.

When Henry walked in the door, he said, "Boy, that
sure smells good in here, Walter. What've we got for
supper?"

"Oh, I got something that you have never eaten
before." I answered. "What is that?" he asked.

I took the towel off the dish and said, "My dear
brother, this is a dish of fool's quail."

And that is what we lived on that winter, that and what we got out of the garden. And that was the way it was during the great depression.

CHAPTER 18

KEEPING UP APPREARANCES

A Close Shave

It was in the middle of the winter and it was as cold as kraut outside, but it was fairly warm in the house.

My mother said, "Walter, I'm taking the two girls and we are going over to the neighbors. While we're gone I want you to take a bath. You smell like a billy goat."

You see, it had been a couple of weeks since I had taken a bath and I will admit I was pretty grubby.

She said, "Now, don't just take a canary splash or a dirty dip. Wash yourself good and use lot's of soap. There is a lot of hot water on the cook stove. There is some in the teakettle and there is some in the dishpan and it is almost boiling. That ought to be enough."

You see, there was no bath tub in the house. For that matter, there was no bathroom at all and when we had to go, we went outside to the little tin house in back yard. And when we had to take a bath we went outside and got the number two washtub and brought it in the house, in the kitchen by the nice warm fire. That is, if there was no one in the house but me. If my little sisters were anywhere around, it was impossible for anyone to get me to take a bath. This was the reason for the visit to the neighbors.

Well, as soon as I thought it was safe, I got the wash tub down and put it in the kitchen and started with the hot water. Then I added enough cold water to make it just right. I grabbed a bar of soap. We never had any of that good smelling store boughten bath soap. We all used Fels Naptha soap. That is a brown looking soap that smells a little like kerosene.

I sure hated to take a bath in the winter time. It was fun in the summer. We always went down to the well and took a bath in the cow trough and that was far enough away from the house that the girls couldn't see me.

Well, I took all of my clothes off and was a standing in the tub trying to wash the top half first. I was too big to sit down in the tub. I struggled through it 'til I thought I was pretty clean. I had begun to smell a little better, anyway.

Then the thought ran through my mind, "I still have a few minutes 'fore they are likely to be back. I think I'll try to shave. I've never done that before and I bet that would be a lot of fun."

So as soon as I had gotten on my clean clothes and had dumped out the water from the wash tub, I took that bar of Fels Naptha soap and the wash rag and lathered my face up good. Then I went and got my dad's straight razor and went over to the dresser. That was the only place that there was a mirror.

I knew that I didn't have too much time so whatever I was a going to do I would have to do it real fast.

As I shaved I couldn't figure out why I couldn't make that same sound that my dad did when he shaved. Finally, I came to the conclusion that the reason was that I didn't have any whiskers.

When I went to wash the soap off the razor, I noticed

that it was a little pink and my face was a stinging and smarting real good.

By now, I heard the car a coming in the distance and I hurried real fast and washed my face real good. But first I took time to put my dad's razor away and I was still a washing my face when my mother came in.

She noticed that the water was a little pink and my face was real red.

Then she said, "Walter, I wanted you to scrub good, but I didn't expect you to take the hide off."

New Shoes

I was getting close to fifteen years old. I had gone barefooted all summer long, but now it was stating to get a little cold. In fact, it was past time for me to have a pair of shoes. My dad had kept putting it off 'cause he just plain didn't have the money.

Well, the neighbors brought over a big box of clothes full of some hand – me – downs, and in it was several pairs of shoes. But you know what? There was not a one of them that was big enough to fit me. To say the least, I was very disappointed. There was something for all of the rest of the kids except me. Oh, there was some pants that were a little big and a coat that looked pretty good, but still, that did not do my feet any good. So my dad told my mother to take me to Bisbee and get me a pair of shoes and he gave her two dollars.

Well, I put on those pants and that coat and spent an hour a washing my feet, 'cause they were in pretty bad shape. My mother said that she wouldn't take me to town if my feet were the least bit dirty. When you go barefooted all summer it is next to impossible to get your feet that clean, but I tried and after a while they passed my mother's inspection and we were on our way.

We parked by the Bisbee Post Office and walked up the street towards the Penney's Store. That sidewalk was sure cold and I was still barefooted. I had on those pants that were too big for me and the coat that didn't fit any better. And what made it worse was that I was so tall that my mother could stand under my arm and not even touch it. People were a looking at me and some of them were a laughing. Boy! Was I ever embarrassed!

When we walked into the Penney's Store, the clerk held his hand over his mouth so that we could not see him a laughing.

He said to my mother, "May I help you?"

She said, "You can if you've got a big pair of shoes for this boy of mine."

He brought out six pairs of the biggest shoes that he had and they didn't come close to fitting.

Then he said, "I am sorry. That is all I have, mam. You might try the P. D. Store. They might have something that will fit him."

So we went down there and they didn't have anything, either. I was beginning to think that I was going to have to go around all winter without any shoes.

As we started out the door, I noticed that there was a pair of shoes in the window on display that were whoppers, and I said to my mother, "Look at them shoes in the window. I'll bet they'll fit!"

The reason that they looked so big was 'cause they were setting right next to a real small pair.

I said, "Mamma, why don't you go in and see if he will sell them to us?" So she did.

The clerk said, "Why, I guess so. Just a minute. I'll go and see what the manager has to say about it." He was back in a minute with a big smile on his face.

He said, "The boss said that it is OK to sell them."

So he got them out of the window and I tried them on and they fit just perfect.

Then Mamma asked, "How much are they?"

"Well," he said, "there is nobody that I know of around here that can wear them, so I will let you have them for a dollar."

So Mamma gave him a dollar and we were on our way back home.

Boy, I sure took good care of them 'cause I didn't know when I would ever find a pair of fourteens again.

The Circus

I had gotten up extra early one morning to look at some rabbit traps that I had set the night before. Much to my delight there were five rabbits in the whole lot of them. So I went about skinning them and getting them ready for the skillet, when I saw, to the south about a mile, a circus train. It was a big one for our little town.

I stood there and watched 'til it was out of sight and then went into the house with my rabbits and put them on the kitchen table.

Daddy was just getting up.

"Well, Walter, it looks like you hit the jackpot last night." He said.

But I was not as enthused as he thought I should be and he guessed what I was a thinking.

He knew about the circus coming to town that day so he said, "Don't you go to that circus today. You stay at school and don't play hookey."

He'd guessed right, but I replied that I would do as he said, then started out to do my chores and get ready for school

We had about a mile to walk to where the bus would pick us up, so I had to allow myself enough time to get there before the bus did.

On this particular morning, I got to the bus stop extra early and I waited and waited and the longer I waited the hungrier I got. So I ate one of my sandwiches, then another. Soon they were all gone.

Then I started in on my cake and I slicked it all up and wiped my face off with my shirt sleeve and said, "Well, I guess that I won't have to be bothered with that any more, but doggonit, I'm still hungry."

About that time the bus came along.

As I stepped into the bus the driver said, "Did you forget your lunch?"

"Naw, I was hungry and I ate it." I answered.

I was the last kid to get on and the bus was pretty full. I had to find a seat the best that I could.

As I sat down, all the talk that I heard was about the circus and it sounded like every body was going. That is, everybody except me. I was so down in the mouth that I looked as if I had a double chin.

As soon as the bus stopped, most all of the boys headed for the circus grounds that were across the street from the school, in a clearing that had been cleaned off.

I went in to the school yard and started playing marbles with some of the little kids 'til it was time for school to start.

When the bell rang, I went in and took my seat and looked around. It looked like it was a school for girls instead of a regular grade school. There were a few boys that were too little to work for the circus there, but that was all.

The teacher, who was Miss York, was thoroughly disgusted that so many of the boys were gone.

She said, "Where are all of the boys this morning?" as if she didn't know.

At that moment, Mr. Rouse, the principal, walked in. His eye caught mine and all he said was, "Walt, you go to the office." Which I did with pleasure.

He stayed in the classroom for a few minutes and then came into his office where I was a waiting for him.

He slapped me on the shoulder and asked, "Why are you in school today?"

And I said, "Well, there are two reasons and one of them is that my dad told me not to play hookey and the other one is that I wouldn't want you to get mad at me for something like that."

"I'm glad to see what you're at school, anyway. All of the boys that have gone to the circus without per – mission will have to come back to school."

He sat down right then and wrote me out an excuse from school and handed it to me and said, "Go and have a good time and I'll explain it to your dad if you get in trouble." So off I went to the circus grounds.

There was a big guy with a half dozen kids a following him around and as he came past me he said, "Do you want to work?"

I answered, "I sure do!"

He asked, "What's your name? Mine is Blacky."

He was not black from being born that way, but that was circus dirt on him and he was as tough as rawhide and just as mean. The way he hollered at those kids was a fright. But he seemed to like me because I was big and willing to do anything he told me to do.

Well, we finally got the tent up and after all of the work was done, he said, "Walt, come over here and I'll get your tickets. How many are there of you kids?"

I said that there were five and my mother and dad. So he handed me a whole hand full of tickets and told me that they were good at either the afternoon or the night performance.

I felt as rich as a Wall Street banker and I stuffed them in my pocket and headed for the school to clean up.

When I saw myself in the mirror, I looked just like Blacky and the white shirt I had on was a mess.

Well, I got most of the dirt off and said to myself,
"I'll take in the afternoon show. Then I'll go again
tonight with my folks."

It was about time for the afternoon show to start so
I went up to the window and gave them one of my tickets.

The man said, "That will eighty – seven cents,
please." I had a feeling that I had been robbed and was so
mad that I felt like tearing up the tickets and throwing
them in his face.

I stood there a few minutes, then slowly walked away,
dragging my toes in the dust as I went.

I always went with the idea that circuses were some –
thing wonderful and now my idea exploded in my face. I
was not too sure what my folks would say, either. All I
could do now was to go back to school.

There was about an hour of school left, but did I go
in and finish the rest of the day? **NO, sir!** I just sat
outside on the steps. Why should a guy go to school when
he had an excuse in his pocket, especially when it was
from the principal.

I thought that some of the kids could see me, so I
took the circus tickets out of my pocket and put them in a
little pile on the steps beside me so the other kids would
think I was rich.

But I was soon tired of that and put them all back in
my pocket and scooted back up against the building and
wrapped my arms around my legs and put my chin on my knees
to wait 'til school was out. I was getting mighty hungry,
too, since I had eaten my lunch before I ever got on the
bus.

Pretty soon the bell rang and here came the kids like
a bunch of wild burros. Five of the bigger kids stopped
where I was sitting. One of them asked, with a very
envious tone of voice, "Where did you get those tickets?"

I pulled my excuse from my pocket and showed it to
them and said, "I worked for them."

212

Then they all turned and went slouching off saying,
"He's a teacher's pet."

Those were fighting words in my book and I was down
off of those steps and had that big guy by the collar
before you could count your marbles and the fight was on.
And it was a good one, too.

In this particular one, I came out best man, but when
I was through my shirt was torn half off and I looked like
a mess.

The bus was a coming around the corner by then and I
was glad, 'cause I had had a pretty rugged day of it.
There were a few of the kids ahead of me, but I was able
to get a good seat by the window, anyway.

When I had adjusted myself in the seat, a bunch of
the kids started to ask me a lot of questions about the
fight.

All I said was, "I won it!" And that was mostly
what they were interested in, anyway.

I was the first one off the bus. As I started
walking home that seemed like the longest mile ahead of me
that I ever saw. But by the time I had gotten half way
home, my mother came along in the Model T and picked me up
and I was sure glad.

As soon as I got in the car she started jumping all
over me for getting into a fight and tearing my shirt. I
just sat there and listened 'til she was through and then
I pulled out those tickets and a big smile came over her
face, for she was as big of a kid as we were when it came
to circuses.

When she saw all of those tickets, she forgave me of
the torn shirt and said, "I can sew it up and it will be
as good as new."

"Can we go to the circus, Mamma, Huh, Please?" I
asked. I had worked hard for those tickets and I didn't
want them to go to waste and she would more likely say yes
than my dad would.

So she said, "I suppose so." And that meant "yes" if Daddy would OK the idea.

When we drove up in the front yard, my dad was no where around so I quickly changed my shirt and washed my face. Then I went into the kitchen and got me a hunk of homemade bread half the size of my foot and smeared some cream on it from one of the milk jars and started outside for some wood to cook supper with.

There was but one thing that was bigger than my feet and that was my appetite.

Well, I filled the wood box with wood and went in the front room to pretend to study my lessons and make the way as clear as I could for going to the circus.

I studied my lessons there for a long time, and do you know, they were starting to take a hold.

I looked over my shoulder and there was my dad a standing there a watching me.

He said, "Atta boy! Some day you'll make it."

Things were going along nicely, just as I had planned them. So I approached him about the circus. He was not too agreeable and was half sore that I had gone and worked when he had told me not to.

Well, we all had our supper and by then he was feeling pretty good. The "maybe" became "yes". So we all put on our good clothes and were off for the circus.

I handed all of the tickets to Daddy and we all followed him, in single file.

When he came to the window, I was scared and held my breath when that guy said, "Eighty – seven cents, please."

Daddy got mad and called the ticket men everything that wasn't nice.

Then my mother came to the rescue and said, "Go ahead and give him the money, Bert. Walter worked hard for those tickets and they will go to waste if you don't."

So Daddy gave the man the eighty – seven cents, but grumbled about it all the way to our seats to watch the circus.

We sure did enjoy that circus! When I saw my brothers' and sisters' faces shine when they watched the clowns and elephants and tigers, it made all my hard work and worry seem worth every effort I had made. And I was glad.

Graduation From The Eight Grade

The year 1932 was a year that I will never forget. Many things happened that year. First off, I was still a going to the Greenway School. I had been going there so long that I had begun to feel as though I was the grandpa around there. I had my name carved in half of the desks at that school. Any of the teachers around there, that is, those that were still there, knew me real well. I was the biggest kid in the school, six feet plus, and fifteen years old.

I had been there so long that the kids had started to call me "Grandpa". That was after I had found a hat along the side of the road and started wearing it. This made me mad and I was ready to fight. A lot of the times the kids would come up behind me and knock my hat off, and that started a fight, too.

This was the last year that I ever went to school and the teachers really tried to teach me something, but I tried not to learn just as hard.

One day one of my teachers had me stay in at recess. She sat me down and talked to me.

She said, "Walter, if you don't get in and study, at least learn to spell and read and write a little. When you grow up it will haunt you like a ghost the rest of your life. Walter, don't you see what I am trying to tell you? All of this that I am trying to teach you is a tool that you will need all the rest of your life. Every time

215

you do anything you will be using some of it."

Well, all of this fell on deaf ears and I just sat
there 'til she was through talking to me.

Then she said, "Write your name on the blackboard as
you want it to be on your diploma."

This made me feel real good. That meant that I was
going to pass the eighth grade and that the next week I
would get my diploma. I would be out of school forever.

We were kind of poor and things were really bad about
now and this bothered my mother. My shoes were all worn
out and my clothes were not much better. My shirt had
been washed so many times that it was more white looking
than it was blue. My pants had so many patches on them
that they looked like a quilt make into a pair of
britches. But they were going to have to do. There just
wasn't any money to buy new ones.

Well, the time came for the big event. That was the
graduation that took place at the Lowell School. This was
the first year that it was used and we borrowed their
auditorium for our exercises.

There were some thirty kids graduating that night.
The Superintendent of Schools talked to us and the
Principal handed out the diplomas. When our names were
called we would go up to the stage and get our diplomas
and return to our seats. After each kid went up there,
the audience would applaud.

Most of the kids that went up there had on good
clothes and looked pretty nice. Their names were called
off in alphabetical order and I was kind of hating for my
name to come up 'cause I was scared. I didn't like to get
up in front of people.

Well, when my name was called, I was so scared I just
sat there 'til it was called the second time and my mother
headed me in the right direction.

With both hands in my pockets, I went up there and
got my diploma and started back for my seat. Everybody

started a laughing instead of clapping.

I never did figure out whether I was funny or just looked that way.

But there's one thing for sure. I sure did feel homemade that day. But I had finally made it and that was the important thing.

CHAPTER 19

GROWING INTO MANHOOD

Mamma Went To California

School had not been out too long after I had graduated from the eighth grade. All of us kids were a getting pretty good sized and were eating quite a few groceries and times were pretty tough then. So it was decided that my mother would go to work. She looked for a long time before she found a job at the Copper Electric Co. in Lowell. I think she was repairing electric motors.

The people that she was a working for decided to go on a little trip and they wanted my mother to go with them to do most of the driving 'cause both of them were a getting up in years and driving was hard on them. That way they could enjoy their trip a whole lot more if Mamma went with them and she'd get paid for doing it.

So after supper was over and the dishes were done, my mother and dad were a talking it over and it was decided that Mamma could go with them. It would only be for a month and that would be a good vacation for her and we could get by somehow while she was gone.

The trip was to take them to Kansas and a lot of the

middle states, then through Salt Lake City, Utah, and Southern California, then back home.

We would get post cards from her from time to time. One day we got a post card from her for each of us five kids, and there was a little bag of salt on each one of them from the great Salt lake. Every day I would suck on mine a little 'til it was all gone.

One day, my dad got a letter from my mother asking him to send the two girls out to her. She was in southern California. At the time, Hazel was fourteen and Rosa May was eight.

I never will forget the hurt look Daddy had on his face when he read that letter. I do believe that he saw in that letter that Mamma had fallen in love with southern California.

So that afternoon he went to town and bought himself a suit of clothes and the girls some pretty dresses and headed out to the coast on the train. He left me 'n Henry home with Oliver, our little brother. He said that he would be back in a week or so and for us to be good and not fight and not try any experiments.

The last thing that he said was, "Henry, you are the boss. See to it that Walter minds you and if he doesn't, I'll take care of him when I get back home."

Oh Boy! Was I ever big – brothered all the time that they were gone. It got so bad that I wouldn't do anything that he asked me to do. So Henry decided to bribe me a little.

He said, "Walter, if you will do the dishes, I'll take you over to the airport and teach you how to drive the Model T." That sounded good to me and things were a lot better then.

I think the reason he took me to the airport was 'cause there was a lot of room there and there was no danger of me a hitting something and he wouldn't get into trouble for it.

He would take a tire tool and draw a crooked line on
the ground for a long ways and then he would crank up the
Model T and put me behind the wheel and say, "Walter,
follow that line."

And as soon as I didn't, he would holler at me. I
didn't care too much. I got to drive and it was a lot of
fun and made the time go faster.

It wasn't long 'til one day Daddy and Mamma pulled
into the yard a driving a second hand Buick, with the two
girls. We were real glad to see them. Mamma had a lot of
trinkets that she had gotten along the way for all of us
kids, but I sensed a change in my mother that I couldn't
explain.

It wasn't too long after that, that I came upon my
mother and dad discussing the situation. They were so
involved in what they were a saying that they never
noticed me a sitting there a listening to them. And this
is how it went.

Mamma said, "Bert, there is nothing here for anyone
except jackrabbits. All you have here is rocks and
mesquite, thorns and brush, and the wind that blows sand
into the house. You have to walk a mile to get a drink of
water and it's mighty cold when you are a sitting on that
two holer a reading the Sears 'n Roebuck catalog. You
can't go outside at night unless you want to get bit by a
rattlesnake. When you want a little hot water to take a
bath with, you first have to go get some wood, then build
a fire and go to the well and get some water. By then you
are all out of the notion of taking a bath. It is just
not worth it, Bert."

Then my mother stopped a talking for a while and my
dad started a talking and this is the way that went.

Daddy said, "Olive, if you go out there you got to
watch out for all of the cars or you will get killed. You
can tell what the neighbors are having for supper just by
the smell. The noise of all of those cars a going up and

down the street will drive you crazy, not to say anything about all of the smoke that they make. People are so busy that they don't have time to stop and chew the fat with you a little. The water tastes like it has medicine in it. And you can't sleep at night for the noise from the neighbors next door that are drunk.

"But if this is what you want, I love you so much that I will help you get it."

It was not too long after that, that Mamma was headed for the coast with my little sister, Rosa May. By now, Hazel was married and a living up in Warren.

My mother dearly loved the coast and my dad dearly loved the old homestead and the two of them loved each other, but the call of southern California was too great for Mamma and that was where she had to be. And the old homestead was all my dad had. It was what he had worked for all of his life and it was a part of him that no one could take from him.

Many was the time that I would see him by himself a sitting down with his face in his hands and his elbows on his knees a crying and longing for the sight of my mother, but somehow they grew farther and farther apart 'til there was no hope of ever getting them back together again and finally, they were divorced.

And that was the saddest day of my whole life. It still hurts when I think about it 'til this day.

Selling Honey

By now I could drive the Model T pretty good, that is when Henry wasn't a passenger. Then I did everything wrong, but when I was by myself, I did pretty good. At least I could keep it on the road.

I was like a lot of other kids that had just learned to drive. I would find every excuse to drive somewhere

221

that I could. One morning I thought of somewhere that I could go and that was to the city dump some eight miles away. Maybe I could find some good junk. That is, if someone else didn't get there first.

Well, my dad reluctantly gave his OK and off I went before Henry could decide that he wanted to go, too. If he went I wouldn't get to drive. It was twice as much fun if I could go by myself.

It wasn't long 'til I was at the dump and there was no one else there. That is, except for one truck that was a dumping off garbage. So I stayed back a little ways 'til he left, then I started a pawing it over to see what I could find.

It was mostly papers and tin cans, but under it all there were several cases of good Mason jars. So I started loading them up and as soon as I got all that fit in the Model T, I was on my way home.

Now, what was I going to do with all of those jars? And that would be the first thing that my dad would ask me, so I had to think of something to tell him to justify the trip to the dump.

Then it came to me, "I know what I'll do. I'll fill them with honey and sell them in town. Then I can drive the car a lot more."

By the time that I had gotten home, my dad was in on the bed a taking a nap and Henry had the job of keeping the flies off of him while he was a sleeping. This was a job that none of us liked to do.

Henry would have big – brothered me about now, but he was afraid to 'cause he might wake up Daddy and then he'd be real grouchy.

So I went outside and started to unload my treasure by the tin shanty.

I looked those Mason jars over a little closer and most of them were all clean and had the lids on them, to boot. It sure wouldn't take much to get them in shape to put honey in.

By the time I had them unloaded, here came Henry and Daddy to see what I had gotten from the dump. And sure enough, that was the first thing that they asked.

"What are you going to do with so many Mason jars?"

But I was ready for them. "Put honey in them." was my reply, "And sell it in town and make some money."

This brought a sarcastic remark from my big brother, but my dad thought it was a good idea and said, "Go after it, Walter."

So I spent the rest of the day a getting the jars ready to put honey in and the next morning Daddy helped me take honey off the bees.

We had a crude way of handling it and it was no easy job to get it all in the jars. In some of them I put some comb honey along with the honey and the others I just put plain honey in.

By now, Henry was a wanting to be included, but I had worked hard for all of this in the first place, so I just pretended that I didn't even notice.

I got ready to go to town. That is, I went and washed my feet and my face and combed my hair 'cause, you see, I didn't have any shoes at that time.

I was getting into the car when Daddy came out of the house and walked toward the car. I thought I had better wait and see what he wanted.

When he got about halfway there he said, "Walter, how much are you going to sell the honey for?"

"Gosh, I don't know." I said. Well, we talked it over and decided to get ten cents a quart for it.

So away I went! I don't believe I was any happier in my life than I was then a going to town by myself and a selling honey. Somehow, I had the idea that everybody that I came to would buy my honey.

At the first house, a sweet little lady came to the door and I asked her if she wanted to buy some honey and she said, "Why, yes. But I don't have any money right now. I can pay you next week."

So I said, "That's OK." and gave her the honey and went on to the next house.

I knocked on the door and as soon as I did, the dog in the back of the house heard me and came a flying around the corner of the house a barking. I dropped that jar of honey and flew for the front gate. I didn't even look back to see if he was friendly. I knew that the lady of that house would not be very friendly as soon as she saw that jar of honey busted on her front step.

I had the Model T a going in no time and I moved over to the other side of town and started a selling there.

A couple of little Mexican kids asked me what I was doing and I told them. They thought that would be fun so they asked if they could help me.

That was a good idea, I thought, so I said that I would give them a jar of honey if they would help me sell the rest of what I had.

I told them, "If, when you knock on the door and they don't have the money, sell it to them on credit and that way we will sell more."

So now we were a covering a lot more houses and all I had to do was to drive the car along and keep them in honey and collect the money as fast as they got it.

Well, in about an hour we were out of honey. I gave the boys their honey that they had earned and started for home.

When I pulled in the front yard, I was met by my dad and he asked me how I had done.

I said, "I sold it all!"

He could hardly believe me.

Well, I took the money and put it on the kitchen table and we counted it. There was five dollars and twenty cents. I had sold a lot more than that, but they hadn't paid me, yet.

"They will pay me next week." I said, "And I almost
got bit by a dog, and as I was leaving, I dropped the jar
of honey on the front porch step, but I got away 'fore
that dog bit me."

Daddy said, "Walter, why didn't you stay and clean
it up?"

"I was too scared of that dog and I was afraid that
the lady might be mad, too. So I thought the best thing
was to get out of there as fast as I could."

"Well, Walter," he said, "That was not the best
thing to do, but I guess by the time you could get back
there it would have been all cleaned up. So it won't do
any good for me to send you there now, but from now on,
when anything like that happens don't leave it for some
one else to clean up. Remember this, Walter, you never
solve a problem by running away from it."

And this lesson has stayed with me the rest of my
life. I never did go back to collect the money for the
jars of honey that I sold on credit. I was too scared.

Breakfast In Town

Me 'n Henry were out in the front yard one day, when
we saw a fancy car a coming our direction. It was a man
from town and he had with him two little girls. I guess
they were about twelve and fourteen. We spent most of our
time a looking at them while he was there a talking to
Daddy, and we didn't pay too much attention to what him
and my dad was a talking about.

As soon as they left I was curious as to what they
were a talking about so I asked my dad. He told me that
the man had a hive of bees and wanted him to come up to
his house and take off the honey the next Saturday.

Then he had a idea.

"Why don't you go up there and take the honey off for

him, Walter? I think that you know enough about bees to
do that." he said.

That was fine with me. Then he gave me some instruc –
tions, which I never heard 'cause I was so excited about
going up there to work on his bees.

Well, Saturday was a long time away and it seemed as
if it would never get there. But it finally did and I was
up at the crack of dawn and was ready to go, but Daddy
talked me into waiting a little while to give them a
chance to get up and have their breakfast.

I guess it was about nine when I got there and rang
the doorbell.

Well, the man came to the door and said, "Hello,
Walter. I thought that your dad was going to be here, but
that's all right. Come on in. We are starting to eat
breakfast. Will you join us?"

I said, "Naw, I had breakfast about sun up. Go
ahead and eat."

Then he said, "I sure wish you would."

I thought to myself, "Boy, that town cooking sure
does smell good."

You see, they were a having hotcakes and bacon and
eggs, and that was all good stuff. All we ever ate for
breakfast was cornmeal mush or hot milk and toast, or
bread, if we were too lazy to make some toast.

Then I said, "I guess I will." And I sat down to
the table.

Boy, was it fancy! They had a pretty cloth on the
table and some little rags to wipe the egg off your face
if you got some on it. And those were the littlest hot
cakes I ever saw. They were about as big as a dollar and
a half. I guess the lady had about a dozen of them cooked
and on a fancy dish that had a lot of pretty flowers on
it. And that bacon was so done that there wasn't much
left to it, but most of the grease was gone.

Well, he passed the hotcakes and said, "Help your –

226

self. Take all you want."

So I did. I took them all and put them on my plate.
Then he passed the bacon and eggs and I took all of them
and started a eating them. I was almost through when I
noticed that they weren't eating.

"Ain't the rest of you a going to eat any breakfast?"
I asked.

And he said, "We will after a while, as soon as we
go to the store."

At that point I was so embarrassed for eating up all
of their breakfast that I could crawl under the table, but
it sure tasted good.

Then I said, "While you all go to the grocery store
I'll take off the honey for you. Get me a pan and a knife
'fore you go and when you get back, it will all be done."

Well, they were gone some half hour or so and while
they were gone I looked that beehive over from top to
bottom and there was not one drop of honey of any kind,
good or bad. So I closed them back up and there I was a
sitting on the steps a waiting when they got back.

When I told him that there wasn't any honey at all on
the bees he asked me what was the matter with them and I
told him that they were in bad shape. They had lost their
queen and had a drone layer in her place and all she could
lay was drone eggs and drones don't bring in honey.

I sure felt sorry for that poor man as disappointed
as he looked.

He pulled a face and said, "Well, I guess that is
that. How much do I owe you?"

I said, "Nothing."

And I was in that Model T and a heading for home
before I could get embarrassed again.

Building A Dam

Daddy had been a working on the W.P.A. for some time
and all we had to eat was what garden we could raise
during the rainy season and, at times, that was pretty
slim, but what he made on the W.P.A. got us by.

Water was a real problem. If we could save some of
it when it rained we would be in pretty good shape, but
getting a dam built then was next to impossible.

One evening at the supper table, Daddy said, "Well,
boys, I think that I can get a tractor with a hoist on it.
I'm not for sure yet, but within a week, I'll know."

Well, me 'n Henry counted the days all that week and
when Daddy came home on Friday, he had the answer. We
were to go pick up the tractor the next day.

I didn't know how he got it or who he got it from,
but the main thing was that we had it. That is, as soon
as we could go over on the Naco Highway and get it.

When we went to get it, we couldn't get it started,
so we wound up a towing it home. We did a little work on
it and it was soon a running. This was real exciting
'cause now we could have a dam to hold the water when it
rained. All we had to do was to get enough gas to run it
on, or at least to start it on, anyway. You see, we could
start it on gas and then switch it over to kerosene.

Getting it started in the morning was a real job most
of the time until we came across a real good idea. That
was to set on fire, an old tire, and drag it under the
tractor with a piece of bailing wire. As soon as the oil
started to burn on the outside of the block, we would pull
the tire out and the tractor would start with the first
crank.

I didn't get to drive it very much 'cause Henry could
do a better job than I could.

By the time a month was up, we had a pretty good dam
built. Although it was not finished, we all started a

hoping for a good rain so we could plant a garden.
It didn't take long 'til our hopes became a reality.
It started a raining one afternoon about two o'clock. At
first it looked as if it wasn't going to amount to much,
but the storm swung back around and this time we got a
real gully washer. In fact, it rained two inches in less
than a half hour.
We were all tickled 'cause the dam was a filling up
real fast and it would soon be a going out the spillway.
Well, as soon as it stopped raining a little, we got
out there in it and were a hollering and having a lot of
fun. I think that all of the desert toads for miles
around there were a hollering, too.
All of a sudden Henry said, "Daddy! I think the dam
is starting to leak!. There in the middle!"
Daddy looked and, sure enough, it was!
He said to me 'n Henry, "Go to the house and get
that old mattress and we'll see if we can save it. If you
hurry, I think we can."
We ran and got the mattress and threw it in the
water. I got on it and then Henry got on it and it held
us both up like a boat. Then, here came Daddy. And as
soon as he got on it, down it went and we had plugged up
the hole. There was no more water a coming out then.
We all shouted for joy, "We did it! We did it!"
So we all went to the house and dried off and were a
sitting down to eat when we could hear a big roaring
sound. When we looked out the window we saw a big hole in
the dam about four feet across and it was but a matter of
a few minutes 'til all of the water in our dam was gone.
"Well, we had fun while it lasted." Daddy said, "I
guess the dirt was not packed good enough, yet."
We tried patching up the hole as soon as it was dry
enough to work the dirt, but the same thing happened the
next time it rained.
One day, while my dad was a working in town, two men

came and got the tractor and towed it away.

Me 'n Henry looked at it a going up the road and felt sad. We looked at each other and said, "Well, there it goes just as mysteriously as it came."

Henry driving the tractor, building the dam.

CHAPTER 20

BECOMING A MAN

A Hunting Incident

Back in the middle '30's summer was all but over and the nights were starting to get a little nippy along towards morning. But the days were still quite warm yet, and all you could hear when the men folks got together was about going deer hunting.

I had been after my dad to take me 'n Henry deer hunting with no success. He was always too busy a doing something or other.

I thought the next best thing was for me to go with someone else who was a going hunting. I knew that Martin was going with his boy and a friend of his was going with them. There sure would be room for me, too. So I asked them if I could go along with them and they said that they would be glad for me to come along.

I was all excited about getting a chance to go deer hunting, so I got my twenty – two rifle out and did a lot of target practicing so if I was to see a deer, I could hit it, 'cause I was not really a good shot and especially if I got excited a little.

Well, deer season was still about a week away and I still hadn't asked Daddy if I could go with Martin. I had put it off 'til the eleventh hour and the fifty – ninth minute to ask him 'cause I knew what he would say but I was a hoping that he would say yes.

But he didn't. His answer was a flat "NO!"

Well, I argued with him a little, that is, as much as I thought that I could get away with.

Finally, he said, "It is not so much that I don't want you to go with them. It's the guns that they are hunting with. They are a pile of junk and I don't want you around them. You might get hurt."

Well, I felt that I could take care of myself pretty good, but there was nothing else for me to do but to forget about it. But I was still a wishing that I could go.

Well, the morning of the opening day, Martin took his boy and his friend up to the Huachuca Mountains real early. He left them there and went back home to deliver his milk. When he finished, he went back to the mountains to join them.

He got there a little before noon and met the friend where they had previously said that they would meet him.

Martin said, "Where's my son? Have you seen him?"

"No, I haven't." he answered, "But I heard a shot about an hour ago down the canyon over there." And he pointed to a formation of rocks. "But I don't know if that was him or not. There are some other hunters up here, too. Or maybe he has a deer and is bringing it in. Who knows?"

"Well, he'll be here pretty soon, I guess." Martin said.

Well, they waited for a couple of hours and finally decided that if he had a deer he had had time to get there with it by then. So they started out a looking for him.

They walked over to where the friend had heard the

shot from the rocks. It took them some time to get there
'cause it was pretty rugged country around there.

Martin got up on a big rock so that he could see a
little better. As soon as he got up there and looked
down, he said, "Oh Lord! How in the world could that have
happened?" in a horrified tone.

The other boy, who was still a little ways away, knew
that there was something wrong.

It was here that Martin found his son draped over a
big granite rock about the size of a car. He had been
shot right through the heart from under his left arm.

You see, what had happened was the gun that he was
using didn't have a trigger guard on it. The boy had
wanted to get up on this big rock to sit there to wait for
the deer to come along. He had stood his gun up at the
bottom of this big boulder and climbed up on the rock.
When he reached for the gun and started to pull it up to
him, the trigger got hooked on the side of the boulder.
The gun was loaded and went off and killed him.

This was a real tragedy. He was a real fine boy. He
had a twin sister and one older sister, but he was the
only boy in the family.

When this news came to my dad, it hurt him almost as
much as it did the boy's dad.

Daddy came to me and put his arm around me and said,
"Walter, now you know why I was worried about you going
with Martin. Remember this. Trouble always casts a
shadow before it. If you are smart, you can see it and
avoid the trouble."

Stoner's Garden

I was getting to the age that I started to comb my
hair a lot and would take a bath at least once a week,
whether I needed it or not, and I would try to keep clean

clothes on most of the time. That was just in case some time a pretty girl might come down there to the ranch. I would watch every car that came over the hill a hoping that this would be the time.

But most of the time it was just Stoner. You see, he was my sister's father – in – law. He came there more often than anybody else did.

Well, this particular day he came to visit us and he noticed that I was all cleaned up. He asked me if I was going somewhere.

And I said, "Naw." kind of bashful like.

He picked it up right there and said, "Walter, you got a girlfriend?"

"No, but I would sure like to have one. Maybe there will be one come down here some day and I want to look good." I answered.

He said, "Well, you look pretty good except you need a good pair of britches. Those are pretty grubby."

I agreed with him whole – heartedly. "But I don't have any money to get any with and I don't know where I can find a job."

"Well, I'll give you one. You can come and work for me pulling weeds in my garden. I'll give you a dollar a day. That is, for a full day, from sun up 'til sun down." he said.

That sounded real good to me and I got my dad's approval.

So Stoner asked, "When do you want to go to work?"

"Right now!" I answered.

"Well, get your bag and a change of clothes." he said. I didn't know that I was a going there to stay with him, but this was even better, yet. You see, Stoner was a gardening a little place down on the San Pedro River close to Hereford. It had an artesian well on it and all you had to do was to open the valve when you needed to water the garden. It was the rainy season at the time and the

234

weeds were really a growing and there was no need for much well water.

Stoner lived in a little two room cement – poured shack with one window and one door, a bed, a wood cook stove, a table, one chair, and a box. Oh, I might say that was a dynamite box that had "*HERCULES*" stamped on the sides of it. That was the *other* chair and that was my place at the table.

He put me up an army cot that was about a foot too short for me. A way in the middle of the night, when he was a snoring so loud that I couldn't sleep, I put all of my covers on the cement floor and finally went to sleep.

I was awakened the next morning by wood a popping in the wood cook stove. He was making breakfast. All I could see on the stove was a pressure cooker and I began to wonder if he was going to start a cooking breakfast.

Then I asked him what we were having for breakfast and he said, "It's almost done, as soon as it gets hot."

"What is it?" I asked.

Then he went into detail to tell me, "You see, Walter, every Sunday I cook this pressure cooker full of goulash."

That was the first time I ever heard that word and I asked, "What is that?"

"Well," he said, "there is turnips, carrots, pota – toes, onions, garlic, hamburger, tomatoes, beans, and a little rice in it. Now, Walter, if you figure it out you can see that there is a complete diet there. So I eat it three times a day and seven days a week. I usually only have to cook it once a week, but with you here, I'll probably have to cook it more often."

Well, I lived on this for about three days then I said, "No, thank you. I will pass." And I went out to the garden to eat my vegetables in the raw, after I had washed most of the dirt off.

Stoner would go to Fort Huachuca every Saturday and

sell vegetables to the colored soldiers. At that time, that is all there were there. Oh, of course, there were a few white officers.

Once in a while he would take me with him, but most of the time he left me at home to pull weeds or whatever there was to do.

One Saturday, the two cows that he had there were getting into the garden and I was having a hard time a keeping them out. As soon as I would get them out, they were right back in again.

When Stoner came home, I told him about it and looked down to the garden, and there they were back in the garden again.

I said, "Those cows are in the garden again, and I just run them out a few minutes ago. I'll go get them out, again."

He said, "There's no need of that, Walter. Just slam the screen door and they will hightail it out of there."

So I slammed the screen door and, sure enough, they did! And this time they stayed out.

I said, "That's the funniest thing I have ever heard of. Why do they do that?"

"Well, I got tired of chasing them out and I would stand here at the door and shoot them with the twelve gauge shot gun loaded with buck shot, and boy, that really makes them move out! I did that a time or two and now they know what it means when they hear the screen door slam."

This cut my work in about half. Every time that they got even close to the garden, I would go to the house and slam the screen door. There was a few times when I got bored a pulling weeds, so I would go to the house and slam the screen door just to see the cows run.

It wasn't long 'til both of them had a calves. They were both as gentle as could be. You could walk up to them and put a rope on them without any trouble.

One day I went up to them to catch the calves and just about the time I had one of them caught, Stoner, without thinking, slammed the screen door. They both took off like a shot and I never could get close to them again.

After staying with Stoner most of the summer. I was getting pretty tired of that goulash and raw turnips and carrots. And I had earned me a little money. Stoner's garden was in pretty good shape and he really didn't need me, so I went home.

On the way home I stopped at the P.D. Store and got me a pair of britches and a new shirt and ordered me some big shoes (which took about two months to come in).

But do you know what? All of the new clothes was wasted. There never was a pretty girl come out to the ranch.

Working At The Jackson Dairy

One day I went to town with my dad. After he had gotten his groceries and whatever else he had gone to town for, he would stand and talk to a bunch of miners who were always in front of the saloon and pool hall in Lowell.

Well, I stayed there for a while and listened to them 'til I got bored. All they were a talking about was the great depression and everybody had a cure for it. So I went to the car and sat down to wait for my dad. While I was a sitting there, down the sidewalk came Mr. Jackson. He was the owner of the Jackson Dairy over near Hereford.

I thought to myself, "I'm a going to ask him for a job. He pays pretty good. Something like $42.50 a month with room and board, I heard. I want a steady job and that would be a good one if I can get it."

So as he got close to the car, I got out and spoke to him. I asked him if he had fired anybody lately and if he

237

needed anyone to milk cows for him.

He let me know real quick that he did not fire anyone, that they had quit if they did not work there any more. This irritated him. I could see that I had said the wrong thing and my chances of getting a job from him were probably pretty slim. But he said for me to meet him there at the saloon in a week. If the boy that he had working for him went to California, he would give me a job.

As soon as my dad came to the car, I told him that I had a steady job a working at the Jackson Dairy and that I would start next week. Well, that was almost the truth, I thought to myself.

So a week from that day, Daddy took me up to Lowell with all of my clothes and blankets. He let me out on the sidewalk in front of the saloon and then he went home.

This gave me an empty feeling inside. Now what was I going to do if I didn't get the job? How was I going to tell Daddy that it was just a maybe job and not a sure thing?

Well, I guess I sat there on the sidewalk for an hour or two a waiting for Mr. Jackson to come out of the saloon. The longer I waited, the more nervous I got. But after a while, he came out.

He was a tall, skinny man that always had a big chew of tobacco in his mouth, but you very rarely saw him spit.

At first, he didn't even see me and was starting to get in his milk truck. I startled him when I spoke to him. I told him that I was ready to go to work. He said that he did not tell me that he had a job for me yet, but if I wanted to work that bad to get in the truck and I could start working as soon as the other boy left for California.

Then I started a feeling a lot better. At least, I didn't have to face my dad and tell him I didn't have a job.

It was quite a long drive out to the dairy. It was
on the other side of Hereford, a little west of the San
Pedro River.

When we got there he took me over to the bunk house
and showed me where I was to put all of my things. Then
he showed me around a little and introduced me to the
other boy who was a working there, but I already knew him.
He went to the Frontier school with me when we lived in
Sulphur Springs Valley. His name was Frank.

I got to talking to him and asked him why he was
quitting a good job like this. He told me that his dad
came and collected his wages every month and he never got
a penny of it, and that was the reason that he was a going
to California. He felt that was a long ways away and his
dad would have a hard time of getting his money out there.

Well, he showed me what cows I was going to milk.
There was a string of them on one side of the barn a mile
long. At least, that is the way it looked to me. There
were eighteen of them and they all had to be milked by
hand. On the other side of the barn there was just as
many cows that another man had to milk.

I asked, "What time do you start a milking these
cows?"

And he said, "We start at 1:30 in the morning and
work until they're all milked. Then we go in the milk
house and bottle the milk and put it on the truck to have
it ready for Mr. Jackson to take to town by seven o'clock.
Then after that we feed the calves and clean the barn.
Then, by that time, it is time to start all over again.
We get through about seven o'clock at night."

I was sure glad that I didn't have to milk all of
those cows the first day by myself. I managed to milk
four of them while Frank milked the rest of them. He was
sure good at it. He had muscles in his arms that could
get the job done.

Well, it was a day or two later that he was a

leaving. He was leaving a few days before the first of the month so that he would have a little money to get him to where he wanted to go before his dad could come and collect his money.

I thought that as soon as he was gone, that I would be able to do his job without too much trouble.

The next morning we were up and at 'em at 1:30 and I started down my string of cows. I was bound and determined that I was going to keep up with the other guy who was a milking the string on the other side of the barn. But after I had milked about six or seven cows, my arms were a cramping and swelled up 'til I couldn't milk another cow. Then the other guy had to come and help me. This made us late a getting the truck ready for town. I was afraid that I was going to get fired, but I didn't.

There was one thing that nobody told me. There was a cow in my string that was a kicker. I found it out that evening when I was about half way through milking her. She didn't want me to milk her any more so she let me have it with her hind foot. Me 'n that bucket went a flying.

Well, I didn't get hurt. Just got a milk bath and laughed at by the other milker.

I said to myself, "That won't happen again! I'll hobble her next time."

I was still a little scared of her yet, but I knew that she couldn't kick this time.

But I was wrong!

This time she kicked with both feet like a mule and I wound up in the gutter with all of the soupy green mess that falls in a little gutter behind the cows in the milking barn.

It was in my hair and down my neck. There was no way that I could continue on the way I was. So I had to take time out to go get the number two wash tub and get some water and take a bath. And that isn't the most pleasant thing to do at 2:00 AM with cold water.

Now we were late again this morning, and this made
Mr. Jackson real grouchy. I think the only reason that
he didn't fire me was that there was nobody else to milk
the cows for him.

After a while I got used to the cows and they got
used to me. I went to work in the morning at 1:30 and
worked until seven at night. The rest of the time I did
not do anything but sleep.

But I had my first real steady job and I was happy
about that.

Two Sacks Of Beans

I didn't work very long for Mr. Jackson. I just
couldn't get by on that little sleep.

I found a job working for a farmer down in the
Sulphur Springs Valley. This was when jobs were hard to
find and the pay was a lot to be desired. You were lucky
if you could make a dollar a day and most of the time it
was more like fifty cents a day, and that was what I was a
making. I worked all summer for this farmer.

Well, when you add fifty cents a day up for over a
period of four months, you will come up with about sixty
dollars or so and that was a lot of money to me. But when
I went to get my pay, the farmer was as broke as I was.

He said, "Walter, I don't have any money to pay you
with. I can give you a little white pig and that is about
all right now. I don't know when I'll have the money to
pay you."

So I took the pig and gave it to my dad to raise.

I went back the next day to see if I would be able to
get a little money, but he was not home. In fact, there
was not a soul there. I was a little unhappy about that,
so I started to look around to see what there was around
there that was worth my sixty dollars.

241

In the barn there was a stack of beans. They were selling for about four dollars a hundred pounds.

I thought to myself, "Here's the answer. I'll take some of those beans for part of my pay."

Well, I loaded up two sacks and they were sure heavy. So I decided that two was all I wanted and I wanted to clear out of there before anyone would see me.

When I got about halfway home, I decided to pull off to the side of the road and unload those beans, just in case I saw the farmer a coming from town and he might want to stop and talk to me. He might see the beans. I felt like I was stealing them, but I was mad at him and felt like I deserved them, all at the same time.

Well, I drove on home, but I was a little hesitant about telling my dad about what I had done, but I finally did. And I asked him if that was stealing. I could tell by the looks on his face that he wanted to handle it just right and make sure that I took it in the right way.

Then he said, "Walter, that is stealing and that is wrong. He didn't pay you, and that is wrong, too. In a sense, that is stealing, too. But, Walter, two wrongs never made a right. If you kept those beans, every time you ate beans you would think about what you had done. And you wouldn't be very happy about that."

"Now what do you want me to do with the beans, Daddy? Shall I take them back or shall I leave them there where I left them and say nothing?" I asked.

He said, "Go get the beans and take them back to him and put them where you got them from."

"But what will I do if he sees me?" I asked. "Shall I tell him that I have stolen some beans from him and I was bringing them back because it got to bothering me?"

"It will be better to do that than to keep them." he said.

Man! I sure hated to do that. I worried all night long about it and what I was going to do.

Well, I got up real early, the next morning, way before it started to get daylight, and drove down the road to where the beans were stashed. I was even worried for fear somebody might have found them and taken them. But they were still there.

So I loaded them in the car and started for the barn where I had gotten them, a hoping all of the time that I could get there before he had gotten up. Maybe the dog would not see me and start a barking.

As I pulled into the front yard, the sun was just starting to come up and it was not quite good light yet.

I thought to myself, "Why in the world do I get myself into these kinds of problems all of the time?"

By now, I felt just like I had robbed a bank and was some kind of a criminal and if I was ever caught that would be the end of everything for me.

Well, I went up to the barn and started to unload the beans and there was not one sack of beans left there! But I got them out of the car in a hurry, all of the time expecting the farmer to walk up to me.

Somehow those beans did not weigh so much this time as they did when I had loaded them up the first time.

I was real fast a getting out of there and as far as I could tell I had made the grade and no one saw me.

I was about even with the front gate when I heard someone holler, "**WALTER!**"

I thought to myself, "Oh no! I have had it now. What am I going to say?"

I stopped and here he came on a trot.

As he came close to the car he said, "I was afraid that you were going to leave before I could pay you what you have coming."

Then he pulled some money out of his shirt pocket and handed it to me.

My face was red and I guess he saw it.

Then he said, "Walter, I did not blame you for

taking those two sacks of beans, but I am proud of you for bringing them back. That makes me feel real good."

He shook my hand and said, "If I ever get in the money, will you come back and work for me?"

Now I felt good!

As soon as I got home and told my dad what had happened, he felt good and was proud of me.

I never did that again! And I have remembered this lesson all the rest of my life. Two wrongs never do make a right!

The Cow Business

The depression of the '30's had started to take its toll pretty heavy and it affected a lot of the small farmers in the southern part of Arizona, particularly the small dairymen with only a few cows. They were finding themselves in a situation where they were not getting enough for their milk to buy feed for their cows. And this was what happened to the neighbor just to the south of us. He found himself in a bind overnight, so to speak. So he came up to see my dad about putting his cows on our pasture.

We almost always had some grass 'cause we didn't pasture it down as low as the rest of the neighbors did. He was willing to make any kind of a deal as long as it didn't take money.

At the time, we didn't have any cows that were a giving milk and it wasn't too hard for the two of them to get together. And this is how it was.

We were to have all of the milk from all of the cows in exchange for what grass they could eat. There were not very many of them. I think there were six, mostly Guernseys and Jerseys. They were real nice cows, nice and gentle and easy to milk. All we did was to put a little feed in a wash tub and they would stand there 'til we were through milking, for the most part.

It was sure good to have a lot of good milk to drink again, to say nothing of the butter and good cream. It was not long 'til we had milk everywhere. The chickens couldn't drink it all and there was a lot of it going to waste. So I suggested that we get some calves to take what we didn't use in the house.

Daddy and Henry thought that this was a good idea, but where was the money coming from to buy the calves? They were not very much, like a couple of dollars or so. But we didn't even have that. So Daddy gave his OK for me to go to some of the dairies around there to see if they were throwing away any of their calves. You could most always get bull calves for nothing, but the heifers, they tried to sell if they could.

When I told them that I was wanting to go into the dairy business some day and this might be a good start for me, some of them gave me a calf and some promised me one.

Well, anyway, we wound up with a few calves to use up some of the surplus milk. It was kind of fun to feed all of those calves and it wasn't long 'til I was attached to them all. I gave them each a name.

Things went along real good. Only half of them got the calf scours and got pretty sick and almost died on us. But we doctored them up with raw hen eggs and a little baking soda and it wasn't long 'til they were all a going along good. That is, 'til a cattle buyer came along and bought off all of the neighbor's cows for practically nothing. But that was still more than we had.

Now, here we were with all of those calves and no milk to feed them. We had two choices. One was to give them away or we could go buy a cheap cow and finish raising them 'til they were big enough to eat grain and hay.

I think my dad saw how much they meant to me 'cause

he went down to Sulphur Springs Valley and bought one cow
and a couple of small heifers. I think he must have
gotten them pretty cheap, for I knew that he didn't have
much money.

The cow that he bought had been a milking for several
years without having a calf. There was something wrong
with her that she never had another calf, but kept right
on a giving milk. She was a big Guernsey with very sharp
horns and she used them on the other cattle when they got
in her way.

Well, she gave enough milk to save the calves 'til
they could get to eating grass and a little grain. Then
they were turned out to pasture and fed a little grain
once a day.

It was my job to draw water for them with a five
gallon bucket from the well. It was some fifty feet deep
and the water stayed about twenty – five feet from the top
most of the time.

One evening, while we were eating supper, Daddy said,
"Walter, I am going to give you all of the calves. And
Henry, I will give you the Guernsey cow. This was fine
with both of us.

I said to Henry, "Now you can draw water for your
cow and I will draw water for my calves." So we
compromised and we both drew the water together.

Henry's cow was nice and fat all of the time. But I
really wasn't very proud of my little calves. They were
pot – bellied and skinny and kind of doggied looking. But
the main thing that mattered to me was that they were
mine.

I got kind of tired of them after a while, though,
and didn't pay too much attention to them 'cause I was
busy a doing other things like cooking, keeping the house
clean, and keeping an eye on our younger brother, Oliver,
while Daddy and Henry worked in town. So it didn't seem
long 'til all of the little heifers were grown and were a

going to have calves, some sooner than the others. There was a need for some kind of a milking barn to take care of them in when they came fresh.

You know how things are when there' no money to do with, so I said, "Why don't we make a barn out of 'dobe? That won't cost anything."

So that is what I spent my time a doing for the next several months, making 'dobe bricks 'til I had made a thousand of them. That was the figure I was shooting for before Daddy would help us lay them up in a wall for a barn. I guess he said that so I would have a goal to work · toward and wouldn't be stopping in the middle of my job.

Well, one Saturday, me 'n Henry and Daddy laid up the walls. Or, I should say we got started. It took several days 'til it was done.

Then there was another problem. What could we use for a roof? We got the walls up but that ain't any good without a roof.

Well, the walls stood there for a long time.

One day I said, "You know that Guernsey heifer looks as if she will have a calf any day now. I have an idea. I don't know what it's worth, but there's an old smoke stack that has blown down over by the Shattuck Den mine that looks as if nobody is going to use . Maybe we could get that for the roof."

Daddy said, "That's a good idea. I'll go see Tom, the manager, in the morning and see if I can get it."

Daddy and Tom were good friends and I knew that it was as good as in the bag as soon as he asked him.

It took us several days to take it apart and get it hauled to the ranch.

Now the next thing was to find some kind of timbers to hold it up.

For that, we went to see Henry C. He was the section foreman for the railroad down at Bisbee Junction. He had some old switch ties that were past use for the railroad and he let us have some of them. You see, they are a lot longer than regular railroad ties.

Well, we brought home several of them and we got the roof on. Then we looked around and managed to get together enough old lumber to build a stanchion. We used a piece of corrugated tin for a trough to hold the feed.

Now we were ready for the heifer to have her calf, and none too soon. She had her calf the very next week.

We sure had a hard time of getting her up to the barn to milk her. She was used to being free in the pasture, which was almost 160 acres. When we finally got her in the stanchion and started to walk up to her to milk her, she started a kicking like a mule. It was impossible to get close enough to milk her.

Daddy said, "We'll have to do something to break her of that."

So he got a coil off of the old Model T and rigged it up to a battery with a wire that touched her on the back.

He said, "Now, Walter, you walk up to her, and Henry, when she starts to kick, you touch the wire on the battery and that will give her a good jolt. Then she will know that we mean business and a few times of that, she will calm down and we can milk her."

Well, this is the way it went.

I walked up to her. She kicked. Henry touched the battery with the wire. She bellowed a little and jumped a little.

"Walter, walk up to her again." Daddy said.

So I did and Henry touched the wire to the battery again. This time she got a good shock and let out a real bellow and backed up and took the whole stanchion with her. She headed for the south forty and we were a running after her. She didn't stop running 'til she couldn't run any more. Then we went up and put a rope around her neck, making sure that we didn't get too close to her hind legs.

Well, we got her to the barn and tied her up to a

post and from the looks of her tits, we would never get
her milked. They were badly scratched up a going through
the brush.

I don't know how we did it, but we finally got her
tied up and got the calf a sucking and got her milked out.

We didn't keep her very long after that 'cause my dad
never liked a kicky cow no matter how much milk she gave.
He sold her to a fellow who ran a dairy for a good price.
He didn't care how much they kicked as long as they gave a
lot of milk. I was sure glad, too, 'cause I hated her and
I knew that I would be the one that would have to milk her
if she stayed around there.

Well, while I was a staying home and doing the
cooking and keeping the house and taking care of the cows,
Daddy and Henry worked in town and made the money. To me,
it seemed like they brought home a lot of money a doing
cement work, plastering, brick work, and whatever they
could find to do.

But I was sure a getting tired of staying home all of
the time by myself a doing housework for those two and our
brother, Oliver. I wanted to trade with them for a while
and I told my dad so.

So he let me work in town for a day or two and Daddy
stayed home and cooked. Boy, that cooking was enough for
me! I was ready to take my job back again even though I
hated it.

One day, they came home with a second – hand Ford V – 8
panel station wagon. It sure looked sharp and I was
admiring it, when Henry said, "I'm glad you like it
'cause it's mine."

Then I was mad and jealous all at the same time, and
I let my dad know how I felt.

"Here I stay home and work like a dog for you two
guys and Henry gets a new car and I get nothing. That
ain't a fair deal!"

"Well, Walter," he said, "I have been buying feed

for your cattle for a long time and they are worth a lot more than the Ford V – 8. I only paid $195 for it.

I said, "I don't care. It's a bum deal just the same."

Then Henry said, "I'll trade you for the cows, if that's what you want."

And I said, "That's what I want!" Now I was out of the cow business!

Henry kept them for a little while and then sold them for close to a thousand dollars.

That taught me a lesson. Don't envy what the other fellow has. It may not be as good as what you have.

These are the heifers I raised, then traded them to Henry for a Ford V – 8 Station Wagon.

This is me with my Ford V – 8 wood – paneled station wagon.

CHAPTER 21

I WAS ON MY OWN

Learning To Plaster

Well, now I had acquired myself a car, a 1934 Ford V – 8 station wagon with wood paneling on the sides. Oh, of course, it was a couple of years or so old, but that didn't make any difference to me. It still looked new to me and I felt rich when I sat behind the wheel and drove it down the road. It was sure different than that old Model T and a lot more fun to drive.

But that didn't last long 'cause I didn't have any money and no job and all the gas I got was what I could bum off my dad and that wasn't a very pleasant thing to do.

So one day I said to myself, "This has to come to a stop. It just ain't no fun to have a car and not be able to drive it anywhere."

At this time Daddy and Henry were a working in town and Daddy was trying to teach Henry how to plaster whenever he had a chance, while I stayed home and did all the cooking and housework, and looking after Oliver.

Well, one day, after I had gotten all of my work

done, I decided to teach myself how to plaster. I got a piece of chicken wire about six feet long and three feet wide and I nailed it to the side of the house with some furring nails. I tried to get it as near the same as you would if you were going to plaster a house. Then, I went and got some sand out of the gully and screened it. Then I got some dirt and screened it, too. Then I mixed the two of them together with water to make a consistency about the same as plaster would be. I put together some home made plastering tools. They were kind of crude, but they were the best that I could do at the time.

Well, I put this concoction on the wall. Then I would scrape it all off and start all over again. I did this all day. Well, that is, 'til it was time for me to get supper for Daddy and Henry and Oliver.

I worked at this for about a week and I felt that I was pretty good at it. Now I was a plasterer! There were a few more things that I needed to learn, but not many. That is what I thought, anyway.

I had heard that there was some plastering a going on in Douglas, some twenty miles to the east of us. And I was sure that I could get a job there if my dad would let me go and try. I spent some time a figuring out what would be the best way to ask him if I could go and see about getting a job.

So the next evening, after supper, I asked him what he thought about me a getting a job. I must have done it right 'cause he didn't hem and haw at all.

In fact, he even gave me five dollars and said, "Here, take this and see what you can do."

When I went to bed that night I laid there a planning what I would say and how I would go about asking for a job. I finally came to the conclusion that there was no best way. Just having the nerve enough to do it was the hardest part.

So the next morning, I got up early and did all of my

chores and got breakfast for everybody.

I got all of my homemade tools and put them in the car and was about ready to leave, when Daddy came out to the car and said, "I think you had better take my plastering tools and leave yours with me. They don't look so good. I can get by with them today 'til we can get some more."

It was about six o'clock by now and this would give me about an hour to get to Douglas to look around a little before it was time that everybody would be starting to work.

Well, I drove up one street and back the next 'til I found some men a plastering on a big house. I drove around the block a few times trying to get up nerve enough to go up and ask for a job. The last time around, I saw a tall man wearing white clothes carrying some mortar into the house in a bucket. So I went up to him and asked him who the boss was and he said that he was the boss.

"What do you want?" he asked.

"A job." I answered.

"You a plasterer?"

"You bet!"

"Then go in there and start spreading."

So I went into the house and took the water hose that was a laying there and started a wetting the walls down. I didn't know what for, but that was what he told me to do, I thought.

In about a minute, here he came and started a hollering and saying some unkind words.

"I told you to come in here and start spreading. Why are you wetting down the walls?"

"I thought that you said to come in here and start a spraying, and so I am spraying. You see, I want to do what you want me to do 'cause I really want this job." I said very sheepishly.

I think that he felt sorry for me at this point,

because he said, "Well, I don't think you're a plasterer,
but maybe you can mix mud and bring it in."

So we went outside and he showed me what he wanted me
to do and how he wanted it mixed. I spent the rest of the
day mixing plaster and carrying it to the plasterers.

When I went home that evening, I was so tired that I
had to stop and rest a couple of times on the way.

When I walked in the house, my dad was a beaming and
looked as if he was real proud of me and he said, "Well,
I see that you were plastering today."

He didn't know that a lot of that plaster on my
clothes was put there by me on purpose, to make a good
impression on him. I didn't have the heart to tell him
that I was not a plastering, but was just a mud mixer.

I told Daddy that I wanted to stay in Douglas because
I was too tired to come the twenty miles home every night.
He gave me some money and I found a place to stay for
$7.50 a week, room and board.

I was making big money now! I was getting four
dollars a day! Boy, did I feel rich and handsome! I had
a **"today I am a man"** feeling.

Booze And Tobacco

The next week end I went home to see Daddy and Henry
and brag a little to let them know how smart I was.

But, you know, somehow my dad didn't see it this way.
Instead, he spent most of the day a telling me things not
to do and most of it was about drinking booze and smoking.

As I left for Douglas, I was still mad, or maybe a
better word for it would be rebellious. I stopped at the
P. D. Store in Warren and bought a bottle of whiskey and a
can of Prince Albert smoking tobacco.

I stopped at the Warren cutoff and dug out the bottle
and took a big snort. Yes, you guessed it, I almost

heaved. It was all that I could do to keep from it. I
didn't want to take that whiskey with me, so I got out and
hid it under a bunch of garbage that someone had dumped
along side of the road.

"There, now I'll know where it is if I ever want to
get drunk." I said to myself.

Then I started for Douglas again. I had gone only a
couple of miles, when I thought of the can of P.A. that I
had bought. So I stopped again and got out the papers and
proceeded to roll me a cigarette.

It was a horrible looking thing, fat in the middle
and to a point on each end. As soon as I lit it, it all
came apart and I had to get out of the car to keep from
getting holes burned in my good britches.

Then I tried it again. This time I used three papers
and not so much tobacco. It looked more like a rolled up
newspaper than it did like a cigarette.

I started a smoking it 'til I began to cough and my
eyes blurred and my head started to swim. And out the
window went the can of P.A., paper, matches and all.

It was some time before I could manage to start for
Douglas again. By the time I got to Paul Spur, all of the
mad was gone and a feeling of remorse had come over me. I
tried to justify myself that if my dad had not made me so
mad I would have never done such a thing.

As far as I know, that bottle of booze is still there
where I hid it. I never went back to see.

Plastering

We had been plastering on a hotel for about a week
and were ready to start putting on the finish coat. I was
an extra man.

The boss said, "Walt, when you get time, fill in all
of the catfaces so when the plasterers get here they won't

have to take the time to fill them in." A catface is an irregularity in the plaster.

It was several days later before I found out what I had done. You see, when the plasterers were working there, they didn't take time to clean out all of the electrical boxes, but instead, they just gouged the plaster a little to mark where there was supposed to be a box. I did such a smooth job of covering them up that you couldn't see where they were.

Oh, Boy! Was the boss ever mad? He said a lot of unkind things. I thought he was going to fire me, but he didn't. He waited 'til he got so drunk that he had a hard time of standing up. Then he did it.

My First Date

It was a beautiful day and one could catch the smell of Sunday dinners a cooking down the street. And where I was a boarding at 1314 13th St. in Douglas dinner was about ready there, too, and I sure had an appetite. I had worked hard all week and was a resting, sitting on the front porch, watching the cars go by and the kids a roller – skating up and down the sidewalk in front of the house.

When the call came that dinner was all ready, I wasted no time a putting myself around a delicious meal and then I felt a lot better.

I went back outside and hadn't any more than gotten sat down, when Cecil came out and sat along side of me. He was the head of the house that I was a staying at.

"Walter," he said, "do you see that little girl a skating on the sidewalk?"

"Yeah." I answered.

"Well, she has been a trying to get you to look at her all day long. She has about wore herself out. Why don't you take her to the show tonight?"

"I have spent all of my money and I'm broke." I said.

"Well," he said, "if I give you two dollars, will you ask her to go to the show with you?"

My face turned red at the thought of asking a girl to go any where with me.

About that time, here she came a walking across the lawn, still on her skates. The closer she got the more I wanted to run, but I couldn't think of a good way to get out of there. So I had to stay.

"My name is Dorothy. What is your name?" she said. "I live down the street two houses. My dad is the barber."

I was still too scared to say anything, yet, so Cecil started talking to her.

"This is Walter." he said, "He is boarding with us here and he's a hod carrier."

She looked at me and said, "Oh, how nice."

After trying real hard, I managed to say, "Would you like to go to the show tonight with me, Dorothy?"

She was so tickled that I thought for a minute, that she was going to hug my neck as she squealed and said, "I will be ready! When do you want to go?"

"About six." I said.

She left, and Cecil 'n me went in the house. Cecil slapped me on the back and said, "I'm proud of you, Walter. Here's two bucks and you don't have to pay me back."

I went in and took a shower and got all slicked up and sat down to wait for Dorothy to come over.

At five – thirty she was a sitting on the front porch a waiting for me. I could see her out there, but I was too scared to go out there and invite her in. Besides being scared, I knew absolutely nothing about what to do when I was around girls.

"me 'n Henry"

You see, from the time that I had left the eighth grade when I was fifteen, 'til now, when I was twenty, I hadn't any more than seen a girl and the closest that I would get to one was across the street. And now I was a going to sit in the same seat with one. I was thrilled, but at the same time scared to death.

I waited in the house 'til it was six, and then I took one more look outside and said to myself, "Boy, she sure is pretty when she gets dolled up."

I went out the front door and got in the car, not even looking at her, and she came a following and got in the other side. I never even said "boo" and neither did she.

I drove down town and parked the station wagon near the front of the theater. I got out and went straight over to the box office and got the tickets and looked around to see what had happened to her.

She was still a sitting in the car. I thought that maybe she had changed her mind and wanted to go home.

So I walked over to the car and asked, "What's the matter with you? Don't you want to go to the show after all?"

She was a looking kind of funny as if I had done something wrong. I hadn't said anything so I knew that was not it. So I asked her, "What's wrong?" And she said,

"A gentleman always opens the car door for a lady when he takes her out to the show."

"Well, you see, I don't know much about girls and I've had no experience. You are my first girl and this is my first date and that is why I didn't open the door for you."

Well, we got in and sat down as the first feature was a starting. It was a love story. The title of it was *Moon Over Miami*. It was a wonderful picture and I did enjoy myself to the fullest. The bug had bitten me and I felt all warm inside and had an unreal feeling, kind of a floating feeling, and I just sat there when the show had ended.

"Are we going home or are you just going to sit there?" she asked.

This really upset me. Sometimes she was so nice and the next minute she was not so nice. But I still liked her and after I took her home I could not go to sleep for thinking of all the dumb things that I had done. Oh, how I wished that I knew what to do and when to do it. I wondered if I'd ever learn.

The next morning at the breakfast table, Cecil asked me how the date went.

I said, "I don't know. I think I am too young to go out with the girls. I am too dumb. I know that much, What is a man supposed to do when he goes to the show with a girl? All I did last night was do the wrong thing. I'm not a going out no more 'til I get a little smarter."

Cecil did something for me then that I have been forever grateful to him for. That was to tell me about girls and what was the proper thing to do and how to be a gentleman. And this has stayed with me all of my life.

Cecil said, "Never do anything that would bring shame to either the girl, you, or your parents. Never go out with a girl that is below your marrying standards."

And that's still pretty good advice for any young man.

The End Of My Beautiful Ford V – 8

It had started to get pretty cold. In fact, it was down right cold at times. I was still a living in Douglas at 1314 13th St. I still had my 1932 Ford V – 8 station wagon and I thought quite a lot of it. It was all that I had to call my own. I would drain the water out of the

radiator every night, faithfully, so that it wouldn't
freeze and bust the head or the radiator. This was before
there was anti – freeze or just the rich people could afford
to buy it for their cars. And that was not me at this
time 'cause I was out of work now and it really was a
chore just to get a few dollars together to buy a little
gas for it when I wanted to go any where.

One morning, there came a knock on the door, and when
I went to answer it, there was a man standing there who
wanted me to go to work for him for a day. I told him to
wait 'til I could get together some kind of a lunch and I
would go with him. I had the lady of the house where I
was a boarding, put me together a lunch. She always made
a better one than I could.

It wasn't long 'til it was ready and just as I
started out the door, here came Dorothy across the yard, a
hollering at me to make sure that I didn't get away before
she could talk to me.

But all she wanted was to borrow my Ford V – 8.

My mouth said, "Sure." but my heart said, "No, don't
do it, Walter! She's just a using you. She doesn't like
you that much to let her go a gallivanting off in the only
car that you have."

The last thing that I said to her was, "Be sure and
put water in the radiator before you start it up."

She said, "Sure, I will."

And she threw me a kiss as she went a floating across
the yard toward her house in her pink and blue bathrobe,
the sight of which would warm the heart of any young man,
especially me, that morning.

I was a working on a tall steep roof that day, and I
was scared to death most of the time I was a working. I
think I spent most of my time a hanging onto something
instead of working.

Well, four – thirty finally came and the boss took me
home and gave me my pay of two dollars. That would buy a

little gas, anyway, I thought.

But when I got home, my Ford V – 8 hadn't gotten there yet, and this puzzled me and bothered me a little 'cause I wanted to go burn up some of the two dollars in it.

I went in the house and ate supper, then went out on the front porch to wait for my car to come home. The longer I waited, the more upset I got, 'til, finally, here it came in low gear and a smoking like it was on fire. I believe it was a going all of five miles per hour.

As soon as it came to a stop, I was there to open the door for Dorothy and before I could say anything, she said, "Walter, I think that there is something wrong with your car. It isn't running very good."

I said, "It looks to me as if it isn't running at all!"

She could see that I was really hurt and was about ready to start a crying any second.

All of a sudden, she put her hand to her mouth and said, "Oh, I forgot to put water in it and I bet that's what's the matter with it. I didn't ruin it, did I? It will be alright when it cools off a little."

Well, that Ford V – 8 cooled off in a little while, but you know, I didn't. My Ford V – 8 station wagon was RUINED!

Afterwards, I sold it to a man from across the line in Old Mexico for $98.56 'cause that was all the money that he had. I wanted a hundred for it, but I figured that it was better to take that than nothing.

To this day I have never seen that car nor that girl again.

The Harley Davidson

I was really sad now. Everywhere I went, I had to walk and 13th street was about ten blocks from the main part of downtown Douglas, so I decided to see if I could find me something a little closer to where I might be a working.

I was a trying to get a job with Taylor and Powell Building Contractors. I went to the office every day to see if there was any openings for me.

This particular morning, one of the bosses came out and asked me if I knew how to finish concrete and I told him that I could. I had done it with my dad many times.

So he said, "You go out with the crew and there will be another man there to work with you. He will be a little late, but you go ahead and mix up the concrete and lay it down. By that time he'll be there."

There was a set of steps, a sidewalk, and a garage floor to be finished. I worked like a horse a helping the other men mix the cement and lay it all down. Then I started a finishing the garage floor and I got it looking pretty nice. Then I started up the sidewalk a working as hard as I could. Still that other man didn't show up. By now, all the rest of the labor crew had gone to do other things and I was a doing my best to keep the cement from getting away from me. I was getting so tired, I could drop, and the cement was getting harder by the minute.

I did the best I could, but finally gave up and went home. Or, I should have said, I started for home on foot, when here came down the street, a man a riding on a Harley Davidson motorcycle. It was an old beat up looking thing with a "for sale" sign on it.

As he went by, I hollered at him. He stopped and I talked to him for a little while and it was not too long 'til I was a riding and he was a walking.

This is the way the deal went. I gave him a hundred dollars and I was to give him the balance as soon as I got paid.

But I got fired the next morning. Not for doing a bad job, but for using bad judgement. I should have started on the steps first and then gone around to the garage that would not have mattered so much.

Well, anyhow, I got paid. I think it was four dollars or so. I thought to myself, "This motorcycle doesn't burn much gas, so I'll fill 'er up and go to Elfrida and see what I can see."

It was a lot of fun a going up the road. Having that wind a hitting me in the face made me feel like I was as free as the breeze. I couldn't ride that motorcycle real good, but I thought I could.

When I got to Elfrida, there was a big rabbit drive a going on. It seems that this went on every year or two. All of the farmers would get together with shot guns, fifty yards apart, for a mile or two and would walk and drive the rabbits ahead of them to a rabbit tight fence some three miles away. The closer to the fence they got, the more excitement there was. I got out there and was a chasing those rabbits with my motorcycle and a having lots of fun. Motorcycles were for me!

When it was all over, I headed for home to the old homestead at Bisbee Junction to see my dad and Henry and show them my Harley Davidson.

When I got there, I found that my mother had come in from California to see us boys. She wasn't staying very long and she asked me if I wanted to go out to California to stay with her.

I was all excited and wanted to go. I had forgotten all about the Harley Davidson and the one hundred dollars I still owed on it 'til I had gotten all the way out to California.

Then I wrote and told the guy to go and get the motorcycle. And that was the last I ever heard of it or my one hundred dollars I had given the man for it.

CHAPTER 22

CALIFORNIA, HERE I COME !

I Arrived

All my life I had heard about the "coast" and what a wonderful place it was and now, in a few minutes, I was to be there, the big city of Los Angeles, California. That is where my mother lived and I was going to stay with her for a while and maybe even get a job and go to work.

The car pulled in the driveway off of a busy street and my mother said, "This is it, Walter! This is where we will be staying. There is plenty of room for you and you can stay as long as you want to."

I was tired from the long trip from Bisbee, Arizona and as soon as Mamma made up a bed for me in the front room on the couch, I was asleep in no time at all. I didn't know anything 'til the next morning when the day — light started to come in the window. I was soon up and had my clothes on and I was ready for the day.

My mother was still sound asleep, so I went out and walked down to the corner of the block to have a look at the big city. Everything was so quiet. There was hardly any activity on the street at all.

This was the first time that I had ever seen a big
city. It seemed so lonesome. There were no mocking birds
a singing, no cottontail rabbits a running around, and
none of the beautiful morning sounds that I was used to
all my life in Arizona. All I could hear was an
occasional car go by and the dogs a barking. There were a
few people on the streets who looked like they needed to
go back to bed and sleep a while.

I stood there 'til the sun came up and then went back
to the house and still, Mamma was asleep. I was getting
hungry so I looked in the kitchen to see what there was to
eat. It was pretty bare. All that I could find was some
eggs and a half loaf of bread that looked as if it was a
week old. So I made a batch of hotcakes and got a glass
of water and that was what I ate for breakfast that first
morning.

By now, it was about seven o'clock and there still
was not much a going on, so I took another walk. This
time I went a little farther, but I stayed on the same
street so that I could find my way back to Mamma's house.

It was foggy and wet and kind of smoky, too. I
walked around for a while 'til I thought it was about
noon. I was hungry again, so I headed for the house.

My mother was just getting up and she said, "What
do you want for breakfast?"

"I have already had breakfast and I'm ready for
dinner. What time is it now?" I said.

"Oh, about eleven, I guess." she answered.

"Mamma, is this the time you get up every day here?"
I asked.

"It is most of the time."

I was starting to not like the big city already.

Mamma had to work from one 'til five in the afternoon
and while she was gone to work, I would look for a job,
with no success at all.

This went on for about a week and I was to the point

that I couldn't stand it any longer. I couldn't see where the "coast" was so all – fired wonderful. This was the most lonesome place I ever was in my whole life and I asked myself what I was doing here, anyway. Why, oh, why did I ever leave Arizona in the first place? And I wished I was back home. Even cooking for Daddy and Henry would have been better than this.

My Trip To Sacramento

A few days later as I was wandering around town, I reached in my pocket and took out my wallet and took a look at what money I had and counted it several times and all I could come up with was eighteen dollars and a little change.

Then the thought went through my head, "Where can I go with this little dab of money?"

As I walked down the next block I found the answer to my question. There on Fifth St. was a big sign that said, "SACRAMENTO $4.75".

"That is where I want to go. No, maybe I'll go to Reno, Nevada. They tell me that there are a lot of pretty girls there." I thought to myself.

So I went inside and said, "I want to go to Reno. What is the fare to there?"

A man sitting in a chair peered over the top of his glasses and said, "You will have to go to Sacramento first, then get your ticket to Reno from there."

"That's OK." I said.

I gave him a five dollar bill and he gave me a ticket and twenty – five cents change and said, "The bus will not leave 'til about five this afternoon."

I looked at the clock and it was about one. That would give me enough time to get all of my stuff and get back up to catch the bus to Sacramento. So I went home

and packed what little I had in my one suitcase and
scribbled a note to my mother that I was a leaving and
signed my name to it. Then I spent the rest of the day a
waiting for the bus to take off.

Well, when it came five o'clock, there was no sign of
the bus a leaving. By now, I knew what he meant when he
said "about" five. It was six before we got under way.

The bus was an old worn out Buick that, when you
started it up, there came out a big cloud of smoke that
you could hardly see through. It didn't look like any bus
I'd ever seen. It looked like a car that someone had cut
in two around its middle, added a couple of seats, then
welded it back together again. I heard somebody say they
called it a "wildcat" bus. But it was cheaper than a
regular bus and that was just what I needed.

There was only one other passenger, a woman, and she
was a crying most of the way there. I never asked her
what was the matter, but I guessed it was some kind of
family trouble.

We traveled all night, stopping several times going
up the "*Grapevine*" on Highway 99, to let the bus cool off
a little. That was all right with me. It gave me a
chance to get a little fresh air and stretch my cramped up
legs.

At daybreak I found myself in the city of Sacramento.
There were a lot of funny little Mexicans on the streets,
or at least, I thought they were Mexicans. I asked a man
standing there by a truck why the Mexicans were so small.
In Arizona they were a lot bigger than that.

"Those are not Mexicans. They're Philipinos. They
work in the fields around here." he answered.

Right here, I could feel the country hick coming out
in me.

I was tired, so I started to look for a place to stay
and see if I could get a job. I walked down the street to
see what I could find, thinking all of the time that this

was the dirtiest place I had ever seen and wondered if all cities were like this.

I saw a sign up ahead that said, "ROOMS BY THE DAY OR BY THE WEEK".

It was up over a second – hand store. So I climbed the stairs and there at the top, behind a desk, was a fat lady in her forties a sitting there. She wasn't the prettiest thing that I had ever seen. She had a hard, tough look about her. She asked me what I wanted and I said that I wanted a room, that I was tired from being up all night and that I wanted to stay there a week or so to see if I could find a job.

She took my money, which was seven dollars for the week, and stuffed it in a little box that was under the table. It was padlocked and had a little slot in the top of it. She used a flat stick to push it down with. Then she showed me to a room.

I was real tired and went to sleep right away. I hadn't been asleep very long, when I was aroused by someone knocking on the door. I slipped on my pants and answered the door.

There stood a different lady wanting to tell me something. I was so sleepy that it took her a while to get me to understand what she meant.

Finally, she came right out and said in a language that I could understand, "My dear boy, you are in a house of ill fame and the police raid this place from time to time and when they come in, if you go down the stairs this way, you will be safe and they will not pick you up."

All of a sudden, I wasn't sleepy any more. I put on my clothes and went to the desk and asked for my money back.

The fat lady said, "Your money back? It's in that locked box and the Madam that runs the joint is the only one that has the key to it. You are just out of luck, my boy."

270

I shook my head and went down the same way that I had come up.

I walked back to where I had gotten off the bus a few hours before. I felt in my pocket and got out my money and counted it. It was getting smaller all of the time, but there was still a little left over after I bought a ticket back to Los Angeles. I had decided that I didn't want to go to Reno, after all. At least Los Angeles was a lot closer to my home in Arizona.

I was ready to go right then, but the bus didn't leave 'til about four in the afternoon. I sat down on my suitcase and buried my face in my hands and made sure that I was where no one could see me and had a good cry.

Oh, how I wished that there was someone around that I knew that I could talk to. I felt that the world was a closing in around me and I was defenseless. I never dreamed that all this could happen so quick. At this moment I would have given anything to be back in Bisbee a hunting jackrabbits in the mesquite brush and getting a good smell of that clean air after a good rain.

After while I looked up at the clock and it was time to go. I don't know where all of the time had gone to. I must have slept for a while.

I wanted to get in the front seat, but it was taken, so the next best thing was the back seat and I knew that I was sure going to get car sick. I always do when I ride in the back seat.

My stay in Sacramento hadn't lasted very long, but it was long enough for me to know that that wasn't where I wanted to be and I knew that I'd feel better a getting closer to home than further away from home.

CHAPTER 23

STOCKTON, CALIFORNIA

I Arrived In Stockton

We headed south out of Sacramento and as soon as we left the city it started to look like a whole new world, a world of farming and fruit trees and grapes. This really took my eye. I had never seen anything like this before and it was beautiful and the smell of the freshly irrigated fields and the blooming alfalfa was wonderful. Yes, I could smell this all over the smoke of the motor of that worn out old Buick.

As we pulled into Lodi, California, I said to the bus driver, "What is the next town?"

And his reply was, "Stockton."

"Would it be possible for me to get off there and catch this same bus in a week or two? I would like to look around a while." I asked.

He was quite obliging and said, "You can stay as long as you want to."

He gave me a little slip of paper and said, "Give this to the driver when you decide to go to Los Angeles."

We soon pulled into Stockton. We turned onto Center

Street and stopped in front of the Weber Hotel just long
enough for me to get out and then he was off for Los
Angeles.

I caught the smell of someone frying steak mingled
with the smell of a pool hall. Looking around I thought
that this place was even dirtier than the one I had been
in in Sacramento. Broken wine bottles were in the gutter
and a few feet from the corner, there was a drunk man
passed out on the sidewalk wallering in his own vomit.
The people that passed by him passed by as if he was not
there. Some of them were so drunk that they didn't know
the difference.

The thought went through my mind, "What can I do for
him. He is still a human being, anyway."

Just then a police car pulled up and the back door
opened and two policemen got out and picked him up and
away they went.

It was suppertime, but I wasn't hungry anymore. The
filth didn't bother me as much as the inconsideration and
the lack of love of mankind.

Then my mind was troubled again and I was all mixed
up as to what I wanted to do. So I walked into the Weber
Hotel and asked for a room and was shown upstairs to room
204 and this is where I spent the night.

The Union Hall And Job Hunting

The next morning found me a little more collected and
I decided to look for a job. This being a strong union
town, I went to the Union Hall on San Joaquin St. It was
upstairs over a real estate office.

As I walked in, I was looked over good by most of the
men to determine if I was a contractor or just another man
looking for a job. I pulled out my union book and this
answered their inquiring minds.

One of them said, "Are you looking for the business
agent of the local?" And I replied that I was.

Then he yelled, "Hey, Mac, there's some bird from
out of town wants to see you."

I waited there for a little while and he didn't come
out. So I walked slowly to the back room. My ears caught
the sound of a poker game a going on and my nose caught
the smell of cigar and cigarette smoke. It was so strong
that it made me cough and my eyes water.

I walked through the door. There were three tables
all surrounded by men of all descriptions and dress. I
knew nothing of the game except that I knew that it was
poker that they were a playing. There was some money in
the middle of the table and frequently one of the players
would rake in the whole pile and then they would start all
over again.

One of the men looked over his shoulder and said,
"Do you want to see me?"

"If you're Mac or the business agent, I do." I
answered. And I handed him my card.

He whiskered his hand with his chin and said,
"There's a lot of men out of work now, but I'll take your
card."

And he wrote my name on a little round tag that had a
hole in it and hung it on the board with all the rest of
the other men's names. But I was the last one on the
board.

"The way this works," he explained, "is this. The
man that is on top of the list goes out first and then
when he comes back he goes on the bottom. That is, if he
is a laborer. If he is a hod carrier the first one in
line will go out first."

By the way that things were a moving, I should get to
go to work in a few days.

As I started down the stairs, up stepped a blonde man
in his late twenties, about five feet nine inches tall,

and he said, "I hear that you are from Arizona. Do you
want to come and share the same room with me? That way we
both can get by a little cheaper."

I thought for a minute and then said, "Well, sure.
Where do you live?"

"Not far from here, just around the corner and a half
a block down."

So I went and paid the man at the Weber Hotel and
moved in with this guy.

I was really getting low on money by now. I had one
dollar and twenty – five cents left, and that was all!

I spent most of my time at the union hall watching
the men pay poker. When the smoke got to me I would go
outside for a while. I didn't want to take any chances of
them a passing me by when anyone called for a man to go to
work.

In three days I was broke except for twenty cents. I
went to the grocery store and got a can of pork and beans
and a jar of peanut butter. The peanut butter was marked
seventeen cents, but I rubbed off part of the seven and
made it look like eleven cents 'cause that was all the
money I had. I felt bad about that, but I was getting
desperate.

I took the can of pork and beans to a baseball lot
southeast of the Santa Fe railroad station and buried it
for a time when I got real hungry. Then I went to my room
and ate on the peanut butter and it made me sick.

As I stepped out of the door, there I was met by the
landlady with her hand out wanting to be paid for the room
rent that was past due. I explained to her that I thought
that the other fellow, Joe, had paid her and that I was
going to pay him when I got a job.

All this did was to irritate her and she told me to
get out. So I got my stuff and got out.

I was heading down to dig up that can of beans and as
I walked by the Weber Hotel, I had an urge to walk in and

sit down to rest for a while and see if there was a
possible chance that I could stay there that night.

I was sitting at the same table that I had sat at
when I wrote my mother a letter some days back and it came
to my mind that this was the address that I gave to her.
If she had answered my letter, it would come to this
hotel.

I didn't have nerve enough to ask the clerk if I
could stay there that night, but I did have nerve enough
to ask if I had any mail. He looked through some letters
and threw one out for me. It was from my mother in Los
Angeles.

I opened it and there was a dollar bill in it and all
she said was for me to use the money to get something to
eat and to hitch – hike back to Los Angeles where she was.

Well, I didn't do either. I looked at the dollar
bill and I caught the smell of someone a frying chicken
and the smell of the bakery a block down the street. My
belly said go and get something to eat and my conscience
said to go pay the landlady for your room rent and the two
of them had quite a battle for a while 'til my conscience
won out and I went to pay my room rent.

As I walked up, I found her a sitting in a chair in
the hall with a dust rag in her hand and a tired worried
look on her face.

Holding the dollar bill in my hand so that she could
see it, I said, "I have part of it. My mother sent it to
me to eat on and hitch – hike back to her in L.A., but I
didn't want to leave until I had paid you. I know that I
owe you a lot more than this, but this is a start."

Her eyes met mine and her head dropped into her hands
that were a holding that dust rag and she started to cry,
using the rag to catch the tears.

I was somewhat bewildered, at first, and wondered
what I had done to cause all of this, 'cause the last time
I saw her she was already to chase me down the stairs with

the broom and now she was a crying.

So I said, "I'll leave this dollar here on the chair and be back with the rest of it when I get it." And I started to leave.

She lifted her head and said, "No! Don't go! I want to talk to you."

Wiping the tears from her face and clearing her throat, she made an attempt to talk to me, but she was all choked up and had to wait a while before she could speak again.

She apologized for breaking down and said that she had two boys and one girl. One of the boys was in the reform school and the other one was running the streets. Her husband had left her and she had to get a job at anything that she could find. She was watching this rooming house while the owners were away on vacation. They would be back soon and then she would have to find something else to do. But she said that she had some money and that she would pay my room rent and I should keep my money and buy myself something to eat. She did not want to be the cause of someone else going bad. She told me to come and move back in, which I did.

I used up that dollar real quick. It lasted one day.

The next day the landlady saw me and said, "Here is twenty – five cents. Go and get something to eat."

I was reluctant to take it, but I finally did. When I left home my dad said if I was always honest, that I would never starve to death. So I had all the faith in the world that I would be alright.

The next day was a day without any food and the next morning, I went to the Union Hall. I was called out on a job working for the Eddie Electric Co. a digging a ditch at the Stockton State Hospital. I worked all that day without anything to eat and was getting a little weak and hungry.

When I came in that night, the business agent saw me

and said, "Are you hungry, kid?"

I replied that I was, but I would get paid in a day or two.

"Come on," he said, "Let's go get something to eat."

We went into the first restaurant we came to and he ordered two T – bone steaks and two glasses of beer.

As soon as they came, I started eating. It sure was good. Then I came to the beer. What was I going to do with that? I had never drank beer before and I didn't want to offend him after he was so kind to me. So I just waited, a hoping that something would happen. And it did.

He said, "Don't you drink beer, kid? Then let me have it." And in three swallows it was down.

When I got back to my rooming house that night there was a telegram for me. It was from my dad. He had wired me thirty dollars.

I took it and paid up the landlady and got a house – keeping room on North American St.

From that time on, I was on my own.

The Union And Trouble

This particular morning, I had gone down to the Union Hall to see how soon I would go to work.

When I got there, there were eight or ten men a standing around and the best that I could gather was that there was some contractor a building some houses out on East Main St. who was non – union. They were all a going out there to talk to him and see if they could persuade him into joining the union.

One of the men said, "Swan, you are a going with us." So we all got into three cars and drove out there to the job site.

Well, I was in the last of the cars to get there and

when we got there, there was a lot of loud talking a going on. It looked to me as if there would soon be a fight, so I stayed back by the car that I had come in and was a watching what was a going on.

It appeared that there was an older man and the two younger men were his boys. The union men were a trying to get them to see things their way. But it was not long 'til there was a big fight a going on. There were fists a flying everywhere.

Just about that time, the older man started for a Model A coupe that had a box built in the back of it, but I could tell that he was not going to the car for some more tools. He reached in back of the seat. As soon as I saw that he was a pulling out a double barreled twelve – gauge sawed – off shot gun, I moved in, but FAST! As soon as he got his arms out of the car, I grabbed him, from the back, about even with his elbows and I put my knee in his back and started putting the pressure on. I told him to drop it or I would have to hurt him and I didn't want to hurt a seventy year old man. So he dropped the gun and as soon as he did, I put my foot on it. I gave him a good shove and he landed on his face.

As soon as I got the gun, I unloaded it and took it apart. I was really worried for a while, for I was afraid that someone would see it and take it away from me before I could get it unloaded. But they were too busy a fighting to notice me.

I put the two shells in my pocket and got as far away from them as I could behind one of the cars. I hadn't any more than gotten there, when I could hear the police sirens and they were a getting closer real fast.

As soon as they stopped, I gave the gun to them and said that I had taken it away from that old man over there.

One of them said, "Okay, you get in that car and sit down."

The police soon stopped the fight. They booked a couple of the men that were a fighting. And they told me to go back to the union hall, but I didn't stay there very long. I headed for my rooming house and stayed there the rest of the day.

It was late that afternoon that I was given a summons to appear in court the next day.

By now, I was really scared to death. Here I was, all by myself, and in trouble through no fault of my own and neither Daddy nor Henry was around there to ask advice from. I worried all night about it and the only thing that made me feel a little better was to think, "All I have to do is to tell the truth and explain just exactly how it all happened and as long as you tell the truth and are honest, that is all you can do and no more."

Well, I got up at day light and got my good clothes on and went down to the front porch to sit and worry some more 'til it got ten o'clock. That was the time that I was to appear before the judge.

It seemed like ten o'clock was a week a getting there. I was a waiting outside of the judges door at 9:30 and as soon as it was opened, I went in and sat down to wait my turn. I knew as sure as I was alive that I was going to have to go to jail.

I was the last one to be heard from and there were others a telling a lot of bad things about me that weren't so and this made me more scared.

When I was called on to take the stand, I could hardly talk, I was so scared.

The judge looked at me and said, "Can you tell me exactly what happened in your own words and leave nothing out?"

So I started in, but was rudely interrupted several times by a loud man. So, finally, the judge said for him to let me finish first, then he could talk.

As soon as I was finished talking, the judge rapped

his gavel and said, "Mr. Swan, you are cleared of any
wrong doing. You may go now."

Man! I was so relieved that the tears started to run
down my face.

I have often thought since then, that there is no
substitute for the truth, no matter how bad things may
look.

The S.R.A.

I had pretty well gotten over the ordeal of that
ruckus that I was involved in out on East Main St. with
the non – union contractors and I went to the hall to wait
around for my turn to go out 'cause I was getting low on
groceries.

While I was a waiting, there stepped up to me, a
tall, skinny, ugly man in his fifties.

He said, "My name is Jones, J. Q. Jones. All of my
friends call me Jonesy."

Well, we talked for some time and I told him that I
was kind of hard up in the course of our conversation.

He said, "Walter, did you ever try to get on at the
S.R.A.?"

I answered, "What's that. I have never even heard
of it."

Then he said, "Why don't you come over to a meeting
that we are having at my house tomorrow night at six
o'clock and you will hear all about it."

So I said, "I'll be there!"

It was down on South Aurora St. in a shaky part of
town and when I walked in, it looked like a boar's nest.
A box stood in the corner and it was full and overflowing
with trash, mostly beer bottles. The floor looked as if
it had been swept some time last month. Dirty curtains
covered the windows. There was a greasy spot about a foot

all the way around the door knob. There were about a
dozen broken down chairs and a few boxes to sit on around
a table that was so wobbly it looked like if you were to
lean on it, it would fall down.

I was the first one there. To say the least, I was
not as ease. I began to wonder if I should be there, at
all.

It wasn't long 'til a lot of other people started a
coming in. They were dressed real well. Some of them
looked to be doctors or lawyers and well – to – do people. I
guess there were as many women as there were men. So I
decided to stay for a while and see what was going to take
place.

When the room was full, they started the meeting.
Some woman was in charge. After she opened the meeting, I
was introduced to all of the rest, but not as Walter Swan.
They gave me the name of "Slim" and everybody else there
went by a different name than was really their own. This
seemed very strange to me.

Well, Jonesy got up and said, "Slim, here, needs a
little help. He is short on groceries. Can you do any –
thing for him?"

The woman in charge said, "Sure."

And she wrote something on a slip of paper and gave
it to me as she said, "Take this to the State Relief
Agency office on East Main St. in the morning and I'll see
you there."

Now I knew what S.R.A. meant. I put it in my pocket
and sat back down on a box and listened to the rest of the
meeting. Most of it I didn't understand. It was not long
'til the room that we were in was filled with smoke so bad
that I had a hard time of breathing. I was sure glad when
I could get out of there.

The next morning, I went to the S.R.A. office as she
had told me to. I was welcomed in and they treated me
very nice. The woman I had met the night before talked to

me for a while. She was smoking all of the time that she
was a talking to me.

She told one of the other girls who was a working in
there to fix me up with a card.

Soon the other girl came back with a card and she
said, "If you will take this card down to the end of Weber
St. every Wednesday and Saturday, you can get $18.50."

Man! This looked like a gold mine to me! This was a
lot more than I was a making out of the union hall. So
the next Wednesday, I went down there and there was a line
of people, in single file, three blocks long a waiting for
this dole.

I thought, "It will be all day before I get up to
the window, but what the heck, I don't have anything else
to do and I sure could use the money."

That next Saturday, I took some pictures of all the
people a waiting in line for this dole and sent them home
to my dad and Henry in Bisbee. All the rest of the week I
spent a fishing and just a loafing. But still, there was
inside of me, something that told me there was something
wrong here. I just plain didn't feel good about what I
was a doing, but at this time I had no other choice.

One day, Jonesy came up to me and said, "Slim, here
is ten dollars. You are a delegate to go to the meeting
in San Francisco. The address is on this piece of paper.
You take notes and report at our next meeting."

I didn't know how come I was chosen to be a delegate,
but I went along with him, anyway.

A couple of days later, I went to San Francisco on a
Greyhound Bus and was there for the meeting. I had a hard
time of getting anything out of it. All I could gather
was that somebody thought that the colored people were a
having trouble with the police and there was something
said about police brutality and how we all should stick
together and help one another with our union problems.

They had a big feed after the meeting and I

Waiting for our dole checks

Me lounging on the front porch of my rooming house.

Me in San Francisco
standing in front of a piece of
cable used to hold up the Bay Bridge.

volunteered to help wash the dishes. And that was a job
and a half! I washed dishes for over and hour and still
there was more a coming in.

After a while I got tired and quit and caught the bus
and went home.

I didn't take any notes of the meeting. I couldn't
have read them, anyhow.

Well, I didn't stay with that group of people very
long. I didn't like the policy they had of making someone
do something that they didn't want to do.

Besides, I had other things on my mind now. I was a
looking for a good girl that I could marry and have a
bunch of kids by.

Me 'n Henry Together Again

I had been a writing letters home to Henry telling
him what a great place that Stockton, California was and
what a good time that I was a having. He was almost ready
to come out to stay with me 'til I sent him the picture of
the long line of people a waiting to get their dole
checks. That easy money, I thought, would appeal to him,
but it had the reverse effect on him. This postponed his
coming for some six months or so.

Then, one day, I got a letter from him saying that he
was a coming out to stay with me in Stockton. This made
me real happy and I was a counting the minutes 'til he got
there on the Greyhound bus.

I believe we talked for ten hours without stopping.
I don't know what we talked about. He would talk a while
'til I got tired of listening, then I would interrupt him
and I would talk 'til he got tired of listening to me and
he would interrupt me. And that went on 'til the early
morning hours when we finally run down.

Jobs were real hard to find and we spent most of our

time a hunting for one. Of course, we both got some of
that dole that was being passed out by the government, but
neither of us liked that kind of money.

Some how or another, I got a job on the State Highway
crew and a little later, Henry got a job at the Stockton
Co – op (a cooperative grocery store) a selling groceries on
North California St.

I was sure glad 'cause we sure did eat good. We had
all kinds of goodies all of the time. I think that Henry
spent most of his day figuring out what goodies he was
going to buy and bring home to eat.

By now, I was a looking as hard for a good girl to
marry as I had been a looking for a job, and Henry was a
helping me look. I think that he wanted me to get married
first, and then, if things went well for me, he was going
to try it.

Well, I found the girl and got married a little ahead
of him by a year or two, and Henry was my best man. My
marriage didn't lessen our friendship for each other.

Henry was a real source of help to me every time I
needed him from the time he first took me to the two – holer
and wiped my bottom and buttoned my britches for me 'til
this very day.

There has never been a greater brother love than me
'n Henry.

THE END